Rigor and Relevance
from Concept to Reality

WILLARD R. DAGGETT

ISBN-0-9656553-6-9

International Center for Leadership in Education
1587 Route 146 • Rexford, New York 12148-1137
(518) 399-2776 • fax (518) 399-7607
info@LeaderEd.com • www.LeaderEd.com

This book is dedicated to my wife, Bonnie, who has provided me tremendous support and guidance both personally and professionally. Without her tireless work behind the scenes, the International Center for Leadership in Education never would have been successful. Her determination to help children has inspired us all.

ABOUT WILLARD R. DAGGETT, ED.D.

Dr. Willard R. Daggett, President of the International Center for Leadership in Education, is recognized worldwide for his proven ability to move education systems towards more rigorous and relevant skills and knowledge for all students. He has assisted a number of states and hundreds of school districts with their school improvement initiatives, many in response to No Child Left Behind and its demanding adequate yearly progress (AYP) provisions. Dr. Daggett has also collaborated with education ministries in several countries and with the Council of Chief State School Officers, the Bill & Melinda Gates Foundation, the National Governors Association, and many other national organizations.

Before founding the International Center for Leadership in Education in 1991, Dr. Daggett was a teacher and administrator at the secondary and postsecondary levels and a director with the New York State Education Department, where he spearheaded restructuring initiatives to focus the state's education system on the skills and knowledge students need in a technological, information-based society.

Dr. Daggett is the creator of the Application Model and Rigor/Relevance Framework, a practical planning and instructional tool for determining the relevance of curriculum and assessment to real-world situations. Dr. Daggett's Rigor/Relevance Framework has become a cornerstone of many school reform efforts throughout the United States.

Dr. Daggett is the author of six books about learning and education, 12 textbooks and numerous research studies, reports, and journal articles. He also serves on a number of advisory boards, including the USA Today Education Advisory Panel.

Dr. Daggett has spoken to hundreds of thousands of educators and education stakeholders in all 50 states. His enlightening, entertaining, and motivating messages have helped his listeners to look at education differently by challenging their assumptions about the purposes, benefits, and effectiveness of American schools. Dr. Daggett inspires his audiences both to embrace what is best about our education system and to make the changes necessary to meet the needs of all students in the 21st century.

Dr. Daggett has been recognized as a distinguished alumnus by both Temple University and the State University at Albany. He received Albany's Excellence in Education Award and Temple University's 2007 Gallery of Success Award.

Dr. Daggett has a special commitment to individuals with disabilities. He and his wife, Bonnie, volunteer their time and lend their support to Wildwood Programs in upstate New York. Wildwood serves the needs of people of all ages who, like their daughter Audrey, have neurological impairments/learning disabilities or autism, by enabling them to become the best that they can be.

CONTENTS

Our Changing World

"Education exists in the largest context of society. When society goes through a fundamental structural change, education too must change if it is to remain viable." This is a statement I have made repeatedly in presentations for more than two decades. What is surprising is how increasingly relevant that statement is with each passing year. The world in general – and America in particular – is being pushed by fundamental changes caused both by globalization and technology. The implication for what students need to know and be able to do is increasingly dramatic.

In 1983, an alarm went off across America when a report entitled *A Nation at Risk* was released. It stated clearly that, technologically, Japan had surpassed America. It went on to state that Japan's technological advancements and the emerging technological advancements of other nations could result in America being surpassed economically as well. If this happened, Americans might no longer enjoy the highest standard of living and quality of life in the world.

At the time that that national report was released, I was working for the New York State Education Department. Our commissioner, Gordon Ambach, was, in many ways, leading the national response to this growing technological and economic threat from Japan. In New York, we created "The Regents Action Plan," a strategic plan to respond to the issues being raised by *A Nation At Risk*. Other states quickly followed with similar action plans to raise academic standards and bring greater focus on improving student performance in our schools.

While we were worried about Japan in 1983, I often thought back to the 1960s, when anything made in Japan was considered inferior. By 1983, however, the Japanese had become world leaders in product quality. How did they *do* that in just two decades? I mused. China and India weren't even seen as competitors in the 1980s; they weren't even on our radar screens. Today, they have become our fiercest economic competitors, and they play by their own rules. How did they do *that* in just two decades? There were and are a number of economic and political factors at play in Japan, China, and India. But one of the most significant forces in the rising of these nations has been how they've shaped their educational systems to meet the needs of a changing world economy.

Who will become our new technological and economic challengers over the next two decades? Where will that leave America? What will happen to our standard of living and quality of life if we can't keep up?

The lessons that the last two decades should have taught Americans is that we need to be increasingly proactive in preparing students for technology that does not yet exist and for competition from foreign sources that are not even on the edge of our radar screen today. As adults, we must recognize that our past is not a prelude to our children's future.

Creation of Rigor and Relevance

In 1983, Commissioner Ambach asked me to work on a team to help figure out how to better position New York State schools to respond to the technological and economic challenges that would be faced individually by our students and collectively by our nation. His charge was to define the problem and then come up with an education plan to better prepare students for those challenges. While holding these discussions throughout the state, I became involved with several national organizations wrestling with similar issues. I also provided consulting services to several other states attempting to address these same issues.

During those experiences, it became apparent that the American education system had well educated, deeply committed, and very competent educators. However, they were often so tied to the traditional education system that it was difficult for them to see solutions that were not derived from the same system that they were both products of and entrenched in. In many ways, every solution continued to be defined based upon the institution's past rather than the students' future needs.

Even as educators we often could not see how it would ever be possible to break from the traditional school calendar, which was based upon an agrarian society whose social and economic structure were no longer dominant. We could not see how we could change the organization of a school day that was built around an industrial assembly line model. We could not see how we could ever improve literacy in our middle schools and high schools even when research clearly showed that we needed to have all teachers become teachers of reading since reading improves when it is taught as part of a content area. We could not see how we possibly could teach foreign languages, other than those that were already being offered in our schools, despite the fact that different foreign languages were going to be the most critical for students to understand and use in the 21st century. We could not see how we possibly could change the keyboard we were asking students to use, even though the common QWERTY keyboard originated with manual typewriters in the 1860s and its use is dramatically slower and less efficient than that of the Dvorak simplified keyboard, which was developed decades later.

It is a long list of the many practices and structures all of us knew logically didn't make sense. However, they were ingrained in the traditional education system, which had become regulated, certified, tenured, and contracted and which had strong school and community traditions supporting it.

A Personal Perspective

While I was spending my days dealing with the educational challenges of school reform, my wife and I were struggling with how to best prepare our five teenagers to become all they were capable of being. Our family could not find easy, blanket solutions to meet the needs of our five children, who ranged in capacity from multiply disabled to gifted and talented, with everything in between. What seemed educationally appropriate for one seemed quite inappropriate educationally for the next.

So, as I worked professionally to lead school reform and personally to prepare my children, both factors led me to pause, step back, and think through what schools could do to best prepare *all* children for the 21st century.

That reflection inspired me in the early 1990s, soon after I founded the International Center for Leadership in Education, to create what is now called the Rigor/Relevance Framework. This tool is now widely used by schools across the nation and in other countries to examine curriculum, instruction and assessment, and it is discussed in detail in Chapter 2.

As my colleagues at the International Center and I began to use the Rigor/Relevance Framework in presentations and discussions around the country, it gained in popularity as a clear yet comprehensive, descriptive understanding of what schools need to do to prepare students for their future. The framework made it easy to see how all young people, my five children included, needed to be prepared to adapt knowledge and experience. Unfortunately, we find schools typically teaching students with a focus on assimilation – as in college prep programs, which offer strong academics but often with little relevance to the curriculum – or straight application, as with many career and technical education programs that stress real-world application but generally do not offer especially sophisticated content.

4

Rigor and relevance are at the foundation of everything we do at the International Center for Leadership and Education. Rigor and relevance together, especially when combined with relationships, form a powerful yet versatile tool that can be easily communicated, both within the educational arena and to the community at large. The idea of rigor and relevance is simple, yet its power can be applied in a variety of settings.

Since the early 1990s – and particularly since the Bill & Melinda Gates Foundation began using these concepts in its work – people across the country have picked up on the importance of rigor and relevance. Yet, although it has become a widely used term, it is seldom fully understood. In this book, we'll discus why rigor and relevance are so critical for 21st century learners.

Rigor and relevance is not a specific curriculum or instructional strategy. It is simply a framework that can be used to evaluate and organize instruction and instructional practices. We find that schools that use rigorous academic instruction but without a great deal of relevance tend to fall into the cyclical trap of teaching it, testing it, and losing it. Case in point: For the teachers reading this, how many of you could today pass an 11th or 12th grade college prep test in a discipline you have never taught? You passed them at one time or you would not be in the profession of education today, but, because the majority of that information is not relevant to your everyday personal or professional lives, you have lost it.

In the world beyond school what matters is not what classes the student took in school or even how he or she performed on a test. What matters is how well a student can apply the knowledge and skill to the world beyond school.

Interestingly enough, what we have found is that when we teach students how to *apply* knowledge, especially in an area they are interested in, they can master academic rigor at a much quicker rate and retain it for far longer than if the academic rigor is taught in isolation. I saw this as a classroom teacher. I saw it as a school administrator. I saw it with my own children, and now I see it with my 10 grandchildren. Relevance makes rigor possible. For example:

- When my football-loving 7-year-old grandson is asked to understand a simple pass play, he can be taught the concept of length, percents, and degrees. Like many 7- and 8-year-old boys, he understands exactly what the following statement means: "Go out 20 feet; go to the left 25 degrees; and I'll hit you on four." That is a simple pass play at Pop Warner football, and kids learn it. To do so, they have to understand length from degrees and percents. Try to teach those concepts to a 1st or 2nd grader from a theoretical perspective, and you will get no where quickly.
- In the arts, you can teach a great deal of math, science, and history to the students who love the arts. To the kids who love environmental science, I can teach sophisticated science and math very quickly, with a high degree of retention on their part.
- To kids in career and tech ed, who like the program they're studying, we can teach sophisticated biochemistry, applied physics, and upper level math skills.

Unfortunately most schools in the country are pulling students out of these programs to double them up in the academic programs – and the students struggle. Our work with successful practices in high performing schools all across this country shows us that this is not an effective way to improve student performance. In fact, it has the opposite impact: it increases student frustration, poor performance, and drop-out rates. Yet it is the most common practice found in many schools, even though there is no research to support the widespread use of this approach.

This is the same sideways thinking that allows the lengthy summer break structure to persist. Nearly every school in the country gives students 10 weeks off in the summer simply because a hundred years ago, kids had to work the fields. But is this structure relevant to our world now? Lengthy summer breaks lead to what is known as a "summer slump" in student performance. To get students to master content and retain it, we must bring greater relevance to their instructional program. Thus relevance makes rigor possible.

Why Rigor and Relevance for *All*

Soon after I founded the International Center, I established its mission: "rigor and relevance for *all* students." All means *all* students.

I have been in every state in America multiple times, and I have visited countless other nations as well. Every time I return to America I am very thankful that I live here. One of the primary reasons for that is that I have concluded that the finest education system in the world is the American public education system.

However, the media and political hype create the perception that our schools are failing. I find that to be a distortion of the reality. Our schools are not failing. They are doing a better job than ever before. Most school districts in the country have actually reduced drop-out rates, and they have done that during a period of time when students have more standards to cover and more tests to pass than ever before. They have done that despite the fact that our student body has become far more diverse. This diversity, which is a strength for the nation, has become a challenge to schools. Thus, we have a group of students that is more difficult to serve and we have more standards and tests, but yet, we are graduating more. That is not a system that is failing. That is a system that is getting better.

The challenge we have is not that schools are getting worse. The real challenge is that the rate of change in improving our schools is occurring at a fraction of the rate of change in society. Technological advances and globalization are occurring at rates four to five times faster than our schools are changing. Therefore, we have a skills gap between where our students are and where they need to be to be.

The skills gap is further defined by the fact that in America we want *all* students to be successfully prepared to become independent. We do that because, unlike most nations that we are being compared with, America has a much deeper commitment to a dual role for our schools. Our dual commitment is to excellence *and* equity. As a parent and grandparent, I am deeply thankful that I live in such a nation. Many nations would not even consider educating, let alone attempt to educate, my two disabled children or some of my grandchildren who struggle with a variety of more subtle disabilities. As parents and grandparents, however, we want all of our children to have the opportunity to become all they are capable of being. This is something unique to America.

Identifying Successful Practices

In the 1990s, as my colleagues and I traveled the nation and the world, we found that schools that were working hard to get everyone to achieve the highest academic standards they possibly could reach. We found that the Rigor/Relevant Framework nicely described the actions they were taking. They were engaged in driving academics into the arts and into career and technical education. They were engaged in driving more real-world applications into the academics. They were moving toward academy approaches in their schools. They were engaged in connecting freshman students in high school with electives that addressed both their areas of interest and the academics needed for success in the 21st century. In effect, we began to see rigor and relevance every where we looked.

We also saw that these schools worked very hard to create personal relationships for each student in their buildings. Students were not numbers in these schools. Teachers and students knew and respected each other. We began to see an emphasis on personal relationships, especially in small learning communities, schools-within-schools, and other organizational changes. This led us, along with the Bill & Melinda Gates Foundation, to add a third factor – relationships – to rigor and relevance, and it is an essential third word in our mantra of successful schools.

As we continued to study successful programs throughout the United States and internationally, we became acutely aware that schools throughout this nation were extremely interested in seeing and experiencing what the highest performing schools in the nation were accomplishing. How were some schools with high levels of poverty outperforming much more affluent schools? Why were some schools – be they urban, suburban or rural – doing so much better than their geographically or demographically comparable counterparts?

This led to our commitment to identifying, researching, and then showcasing the nation's most successful practices. Over the last decade, our staff has grown dramatically. We have created a network of seasoned, highly respected educators and researchers across the nation. Our team finds and evaluates the nation's most successful practices and then shares these practices in a wide variety of forums. From an annual Model Schools Conference that thousands of people attend each year, to national symposiums, to state and regional model schools conferences, to a growing list of resource kits, to a large team of master teachers and senior consultants, we are now spreading across this nation the most successful practices we can find and validate. We make little claim for the success of these schools. We simply were given the unique opportunity to find them, research them, and share their strategies.

This book provides an overview of what these most successful schools and practices look like. It is broken into eight major components. The components are not necessarily sequential or self-standing. They are eight general organizers of the principles and characteristics found in our nation's most successful schools, and they help answer the question, "How can we prepare our students for the 21st century?"

CHAPTER ONE

Embrace a Common Vision and Goals:

Rigor, Relevance, and Relationships for All Students

There is a skills gap in America. Naysayers of public education like to paint this as a failure of schools, but that is not the cause. The cause is the fact that the rate of change in society – pushed by technology and global competition – is four to five times faster than the rate of change in our schools. The failure results from the inability of society in general to mobilize the support and resources schools need to enable them to keep up with the demands of the 21st century.

A quality education prepares students to enter the global economy with the ability to apply what they learned in school to situations that they cannot foresee before graduating. That's where rigor and relevance becomes important (see Chapter 2). A curriculum that is both rigorous and relevant provides the tools students will need in order to be flexible when facing as yet unknown challenges of tomorrow.

Despite all the changes in society, much of today's K-12 curricula are still designed to support what is now an obsolete industrial era. Even school buildings here in the millennium generally look much as they did 50 years ago. And although there have been many efforts to change schools, few of the country's schools have been successful in restructuring their systems process to produce work-ready high school graduates. In fact, in the United States, students appear to be learning the majority of their technology skills in extracurricular settings rather than through formal schooling.

As we decide how to respond to our changing world, we must understand that the rest of the world will not stand still while we think about how to address our challenges. We must remember that no nation has remained the preeminent economic world power for more than a century since the days of the Roman Empire. Spain ruled the 1600s; the Dutch ruled the 1700s; the 1800s were ruled by the British; and in the 1900s, the United States reigned. Who will dominate the 21st century?

A legitimate debate needs to be held about how important it is for us to retain the title of preeminent economic world power. It is worth considering, however, that the most recent generations of Americans believe that what they now have is a birthright. It is hard for most Americans of any generation to comprehend that the poverty line in America would be considered affluent among most nations around the globe. We spend more per year per pet cat or dog than the world spends on average per child. We have forgotten the state of the affairs around the world, and we take our comfortable lifestyle for granted.

So what are schools to do? I believe we need to take a deep breath and take a step back. We need to engage the general community, parents, and educators in the careful examination of what we hope to prepare our graduates (and collectively, our nation) for in the 21st century. As we do that, we need to have a very clear eye toward the future while remembering traditions and history. This entire process will require a systematic approach that begins with a focus on preparing students for *their* future instead of for *our* past.

History Lessons

Recognizing that our children's world today and in the future is different from the one we've grown accustomed to does not mean we cannot learn some lessons from the past.

The United States came to power, in part, because in the past, the nation had the foresight to restructure the education system. Looking back to the late 19th century, America was emerging from an agrarian-based social structure. The rural landscape was home to a large portion of the population, and the vast majority of individuals were self-employed or worked in small companies or on farms. Generally, because of the agrarian focus of our society, most people required only a rudimentary level of education. In fact, most children completed their formal schooling by age 14 in order to begin working full time.

When the Industrial Revolution hit and factories became the country's economic focus, workers flocked to urban centers to seek employment. With the change to an economy based on manufacturing, it became apparent that more leaders were needed to keep pace with the changing climate of business, urban infrastructure, and cultural diversity. These leadership positions were necessary not only in industry, but in government, business, and communities as well. An eighth-grade education was no longer enough.

In 1893, the Committee of Ten was charged with conceptualizing how American schools should be structured to meet the demands of the time. The committee determined a need to raise education standards and extend the years of schooling for a select 15 percent to 20 percent of young people to get them through the equivalent of today's high school level education. Thus, high schools were established, and the committee's recommendations were widely adopted, leading to standardized curricula across the nation.

The committee's "select and sort" methodology was effective. The United States became the best educated and most innovative nation in the world. We were the world leaders in manufacturing throughout most of the 20th century. As the century was coming to a close, however, it was apparent that the United States was not the economic monolith it once had been. America had come to another crossroads. Society was experiencing another significant upheaval in the form of the Information Age. Technology

12

abounded around us, most people were employed in large companies, and we began to see a growing economic threat from other parts of the world. The rise of strong Asian competitors and the loosening of international trade restrictions made it clear that the world was moving toward a truly global economy.

As in the past, the nation looked to education. This prompted the release of 1983's eye-opening report about education, *A Nation at Risk*. Whereas the Committee of Ten promoted a methodology of raising standards for a select few, *A Nation at Risk* accentuated the need to provide *all* students with an academically rigorous and relevant education. This is certainly the direction American education needs to go in; however, we are finding it easy to conceptualize change but difficult to implement it.

Since the release of *A Nation at Risk*, American schools have experienced compounded pressure from political and business leaders throughout the country to raise academic standards across the board for all students. More recently, states have seriously undertaken the implementation of new standards and state assessments to be in compliance with the *No Child Left Behind Act of 2001* (NCLB). NCLB has required every district, school, superintendent, principal, and teacher in this country to look at new and different ways of educating their students if they are to be successful in raising academic standards and meeting student performance targets as defined by the law.

Today, the American public points to education as the answer – or part of the problem. Perhaps added scrutiny of education as a system will help create the spark that ignites a renaissance for America, just as it did more than a century ago when the nation was beginning its march to world prominence. Our accomplishments throughout the 20th century were historic and world-changing, and the United States took tremendous pride in its innovative spirit. But history provides a chain of examples of nations that assumed an elite status as a world power, only to be replaced by the next up-and-comer. Based on the cyclical nature of such transitions and the frenetic pace at which society is changing globally, it is imperative for the United States to consider what actions to take to remain a viable world presence.

Tinkering at the margins will not enable us to achieve our mission of effective change. Schools need to be restructured if they are serious about getting all students to the high standards necessary for them to compete and excel globally.

Preparing Students for the Global Future

There are four major trends – globalization, changing demographics, technology, and changing values and attitudes – that are having, and will continue to have, enormous impacts on the United States in general and on our students in particular. These mega-trends give credence and forewarning of a quietly approaching perfect storm that threatens the middle-class American lifestyle. History is cyclical in the sense that there are good times as well as bad, and each passes. The United States has weathered numerous crises in its relatively brief history. When the perfect storm hits this country full force, we need to be up to the task once again. The students in schools today are a good source of hope and are our nation's most valuable resource. We must empower them to weather the storm.

For several years, the Trends in International Mathematics and Science Study, or TIMSS, has shown American students to be quite average among participating nations. The gap between technology and education continues to widen in America because we are not adapting our educational system to changes in society.

Of course, comparisons of American student performance with other nations are not always fair. Since the Industrial Revolution, the American education system has attempted to balance equity and excellence. Our education system is not perfect in this regard, of course, because all schools are not created equally. Schools in inner cities and rural areas, along with those that have a high-minority, low-income student body, typically experience neither equity nor excellence. In this country, we are dedicated to providing everyone with opportunities for education, although whether we succeed is largely determined at a local level.

Thus, the American education system, like those in Europe and Japan, is open to all children of school age, including those with disabilities. China, on the other hand, does not attempt to provide educational opportunities to all, and economically, it does not need to. China's huge population supplies ample numbers of educated professionals to fill its needs. India is trying to make education available to all of its citizens, and enrollment of Indian children ages 6 to 14 increased to 90 percent in 2005, up from 75 percent in 2000. However, about 75 percent of those students drop out by 8th grade, and 85 percent drop out by 12th grade.

Every country makes a decision about how much of its resources to allocate to education in pursuit of excellence and equity. China has decided to educate a small percentage of its school-age population. India endeavors to educate its entire school-aged population, but is finding it difficult after years of providing schooling just for the elite. Now, India has a deep well of resources to commit to the problem. A Universal Education Incentive Program established in 2001 has a $2.4 billion annual budget for providing students with a meal a day, free textbooks, medical care, and remedial classes. The Indian government enhanced the program by increasing education spending from 3 percent of gross domestic product (GDP) in 2004 to 4 percent in 2005. It is soon expected to reach 6 percent of GDP.

If the United States is to remain a player in the global economy, it needs to – if not budget more for education – spend its education dollars more wisely. Money will only get tighter in the years ahead as Social Security, Medicaid, and Medicare spending reach critical mass. Corporations and other institutions nationwide are reevaluating their payment structures for employee pension plans. Many of these companies look overseas and see the opportunity to move their business to places where wages are lower and employee benefits are nonexistent or minimal in comparison to domestic requirements. If we are to keep jobs in this country, we must take action to provide all of our students with a rigorous and relevant education.

Globalization

Not since the era of the Roman Empire has a nation sustained its position as a world superpower as long as and as dynamically as the United States. From the end of the 19th century through the 20th century, America's ambitious workforce propelled our agricultural, textile, manufacturing, and technology industries to elite status in the world economy. Americans took pride in being number one in just about everything, from inventions such as the telegraph, electric light bulb, and nuclear power to such great accomplishments as being the first to land on the moon. Our ability to innovate still remains unsurpassed.

Times change, however, and cracks are appearing in the veneer surrounding the country's place at the top of the world hierarchy. Throughout the 20th century, the United States held its own as other countries rose up, creating possible challenges to the American way of life. The United States persevered against the German military machine in World War I and World War II, against the Soviet Union and communism in the Cold War, and against Japan in World War II and later as the leader in consumer electronic technology. Although the United States was humbled at times by other nations, such as Vietnam and North Korea, it continued to dominate.

Then came September 11, 2001, a date Americans will never forget. The vision and memory of planes crashing into the World Trade Center, the Pentagon, and the field near Shanksville, Pennsylvania, have changed the way we view ourselves and the world around us.

November 9, 1989, though not immediately recognizable as such, is the date of another significant global event. It is the date the Berlin Wall came down, symbolizing the fall of communism in Eastern Europe. Ironically, the United States played a lead role in bringing about this event and the resulting end of the Soviet Union's political influence in Eastern Europe. Suddenly out from under the shadow of the Iron Curtain, Eastern Europeans elected to embrace capitalist ideals. The floodgates of a free market economy burst open with tremendous force. Several states, nations, and blocs were freed from communism at once, and there was no overarching government to monitor economic development through gradual implementation of measured steps and local experiments.

As economic reform was spreading in Europe, some interesting events also were taking place in Asia, most notably in India. India is viewed as a rising economic superpower today, but as recently as 1991, it was in dire financial straits. The then-newly elected finance minister decided that the only way to save the country from economic ruin was to abolish existing trade controls. Economic liberalization opened India's doors to foreign investors and did away with much of the bureaucratic red tape that had impeded business growth in the past. Before the nation began welcoming foreign trade and investors, its economic growth rate hovered around 3 percent. By 1994, just three years after the reforms, the rate of growth had jumped to 7 percent. Since then, the country has experienced an overall 6 percent growth rate. India had only $1 billion in foreign currency at the time of the reforms; by late 2005, it had an astounding $118 billion.

India began its rise to power by filling a customer service need in the information technology sector: call centers. Call centers employ more than 245,000 there. In America, these jobs are low wage, low skill, and considered low prestige; in India, these jobs have the opposite status. Call centers are indicative of the types of jobs that are perfect for outsourcing. Information technology makes it easy to move work to the worker, and U.S. workers cannot compete in a global economy because they cost too much.

Every year, more major American corporations move at least part of their business overseas to India and places like it. As the skill level of overseas workers continues to increase, more jobs that are considered high-skill, high-wage, and high-prestige in the United States will likely go abroad as well. Outsourcing of the processing of federal income tax returns to India is a prime example. In 2003, roughly 25,000 tax returns were sent to India for processing. The number increased to 100,000 in 2004, and was estimated at 400,000 in 2005. The lesson here is that if the work can be digitized, it can easily be moved anywhere in the world. So doctors in American hospitals, for example, now routinely send digital CT scans to India to be read.

Meanwhile, India also is playing an increasingly important role in information technology innovation. Motorola, Hewlett-Packard, Cisco Systems, and other technology giants rely on their

Indian employees to design software platforms and futuristic multimedia features for next-generation devices. In December 2005, Microsoft announced plans to invest $1.7 billion in India and nearly double its workforce there over four years by adding 3,000 jobs. When making the announcement, Microsoft co-founder Bill Gates said a substantial portion of the investment would be used to design an operating system specifically for India that incorporates nine native languages. The 2004 investment followed $400 million Microsoft invested in the country in 2002. And Microsoft is not alone: Intel will invest more than $1 billion in Indian technology companies over the next five years, while Cisco Systems plans to spend $1.1 billion in India over the next three years, according to company announcements.

The business model that these major U.S. corporations operate under is smart. They recruit and hire world-class talent at a fraction of what an American with comparable skills is willing to work for. From a business perspective, it makes no sense to these companies to support the standard of living of the American middle class. Since Americans cannot afford to work for the same wages as their counterparts in many other countries, the only way to sustain a U.S. middle class is to increase the skill level of all Americans so that they can bring more to the table than foreign competitors. Meeting this goal requires better education standards if the United States is to keep pace.

China is following a path similar to India's. "To get rich is glorious," declared China's leader in 1977, signifying the opening of the world's most populous country to international trade. In China today, there is no question that communist ideology takes a backseat to capitalism for economic growth. China's ascension as an economic empire dwarfs that of the United States during its own rise to power. For the past two decades, China's average annual economic growth has been at an incredible rate of 9.5 percent. If growth continues at that rate, experts project that China's economy may be 75 percent larger than that of the United States by 2050.

Whether or not we are aware of it, China has an impact on our lives in some fashion every day, be it as consumers, sellers, employees, employers, or manufacturers. China leads the world in the number of clothes made and toys assembled. China makes more than 40 percent of all furniture sold in the United States. An estimated 50 percent to 85 percent of Wal-Mart's merchandise comes from abroad range, and the majority of that merchandise is made in China. Furthermore, around 2000, China became the world's largest manufacturer of consumer electronics. In the not-so-distant past, a product labeled "Made in China" would never have been mistaken for a German-made machine, a Japanese-made television, or an American-made cabinet or textile. This is no longer true.

The population of China is about 1.5 billion and growing. Along with opening its economy to free enterprise, the Chinese government made another radical concession: allowing peasants to leave the countryside to search for opportunities in urban areas. Hundreds of millions of farmers and peasants or their offspring have flocked to coastal cities in hopes of making better lives for themselves. China has more than 100 cities with populations of one million people or more. In contrast, the United States has nine, and all of Europe has 36. The lowest estimate of the number of Chinese who moved to the cities equals the *total number* of people in the American workforce.

China and India inspire awe with their size and ability to generate resources. Countries with large populations and cheap labor naturally attract business and enterprise domestically and internationally. China's massive population has allowed it to become the world leader in the production of manufactured goods. The country nurtures its brightest students to become world-class business managers, scientists, and engineers. Plus, in addition to manufactured goods, China has positioned itself to become a world leader in biotechnology and computer manufacturing.

Together, China and India represent a formidable threat to the United States' leadership position in the global marketplace. What makes them more potent together is that their strengths are complementary. China will remain dominant in mass manufacturing, continue to build electronics and heavy industrial plants, and develop its biotech research industry. India will continue its rise as a power in information technology through software design and service as well as its growing precision industry.

The meteoric rise of India and China has happened so quickly that most Americans have not taken time think about what it means to them and their way of life. The United States can take actions to improve its chances of – if not remaining the sole superpower – at least reserving a seat at the head table. The race for the top will be won by the younger generations. Is the American education system investing in its future by preparing students to compete successfully in this race? The answer is a resounding and unsettling "No."

Developing nations in Asia and Eastern Europe place a premium on educating students to excel in industries that will drive the future global marketplace. Thus, when you consider the ability to move work to worker in an age when the majority of jobs exist in the information sector, the fact that India, China, and Eastern Europe are competitive in the global economy is not surprising. It is a situation, however, that few Americans have been able to come to grips with and adapt to.

The rapidity at which technology is changing is another challenge to the U.S. economy. Digital information systems are giving way to bio- and nanotechnologies. Unfortunately, America is not doing very well in recruiting young people to compete for jobs in these technology sectors. While the number of scientists and engineers who graduate from Indian and Chinese universities is increasing, American universities are awarding fewer degrees in the sciences and engineering every year, and of the degrees that are awarded, many are to international students. China and India are churning out large numbers of well-educated students armed with the skills necessary to compete in and drive an economy based on information and technology. In 2005, China produced 3.3 million college graduates, India produced 3.1 million, and the United States produced 1.3 million. All of India's graduates were fluent in English. That same year, 600,000 Chinese students and 350,000 Indian students graduated with degrees in engineering; only 70,000 degrees in that field were awarded to American students. Any American who believes outsourcing of low-skill jobs is the biggest threat to the U.S. labor force is in for a rude awakening.

Thus, while higher education in the United States continues to have excellent standing worldwide, increasing numbers of foreign students are taking their diplomas back home, some because they believe their quality of life will be better and some because they cannot get visas to remain in the United States. Whereas it is the highest honor for a Chinese, Indian, or Eastern European student to land a job in a science or technology field, American students go through the education system with the mindset that becoming an engineer is "uncool." So, not only must American education restructure its standards to reflect relevant skills and knowledge for a global economy, it must also overcome a culture of apathy and complacency that impedes serious education reform.

The United States remains unsurpassed in research and development, but that will change over time if we cannot recruit, educate, and keep talent within our borders. Countries whose economies are growing two or three times faster than ours can offer opportunities for elite students that are too tempting to pass up. The diminishing technological leadership of the United States could signify the beginning of a new world order. The U.S. economy will suffer while traditionally poor countries grow richer, distributing wealth more evenly around the world. As a result, China, India, the poorer countries of Eastern Europe, and the rest of the world will find that they have achieved what they have always envied in the United States: a middle class. In this scenario, the middle-class quality of life to which Americans have become accustomed and which the younger generations expect to achieve as a bare minimum will be history.

In less than two decades – from the Eastern European nations and Russia to India and China – we have witnessed the rapid spread of capitalism to more than half of the world's population. These nations have long envied the potential of what the free enterprise system can provide. Their goal is to emulate America by establishing a prosperous middle class. A century ago, the United States understood challenge and the enormous effort required to become a prosperous nation during a significant time of transition. The Indians, Chinese, and Eastern

Europeans recognize the energy and sacrifices required of them as individuals and realize the benefits of restructuring from industrial-based to information-based societies. These nations are more than willing to put forth the effort needed to attain a middle-class standard of living. But Americans in general, and our youth in particular, seem to believe it is their birthright to enjoy a middle-class lifestyle. They are lulled into a false sense of security and comfort. As a result, we lack the drive needed to match the aggressiveness of other nations in the global economy.

Demographics

America is aging. Americans at the turn of the 20th century typically took their first job at the age of 14. In fact, today's child labor laws were put in place during the Great Depression to prevent young people from taking jobs away from adults. Today, the average age at which an individual takes his or her first full-time job is 18 years, 7 months. The later age of beginning work is attributable to more time spent in the classroom. It is forecasted that the average start age of work will continue to be later and that, by 2100, the average age of first time employment will be about 21 years.

Now let's look at trends in the American retirement age. In 1900, the typical employee worked until he or she died. The average life expectancy was 47 years. Life expectancies began to increase considerably, however, during the 20th century. When Social Security was implemented in the 1930s, retirement age was set at 65, an age still well beyond the average life expectancy.

What the retirement age did accomplish, however, was to keep the American workforce fluid by continually pumping new employees into the jobs vacated by retirees as well as those who died. Today the average retirement age is down to 62 years, but the average life expectancy is up to 77 years. Prolonging life is a result of advancements in healthcare and medicine. Experts in geriatrics and genetics expect the increase in longevity we experienced during the last century to continue throughout this one. Even greater advancements and breakthroughs in healthcare and pharmaceuticals are predicted to keep the average American alive to the unfathomable age of 107 by the year 2100.

22

What implications do these trends suggest? The only trend that remains somewhat static is the current average retirement age, which, as noted, is actually trending down slightly. By the end of this century, if Americans do in fact live to be 107, begin work at age 21, and retire at age 62, the average citizen will have spent more time in retirement than they did working.

Compounding the impending strain on our nation's resources for senior citizens is a declining American birthrate. A zero-base population growth would equate to 2.1 births annually for every 100 women of childbearing age. From the early 1900s until World War II, America averaged three births annually for every 100 women of childbearing age. Social Security was structured on a metric that assumed there would always be more young people than old.

Immediately following World War II, the birth rate soared as the "baby boom" occurred. With 4.6 births annually for every 100 women of childbearing age, the birth rate greatly surpassed the death rate. Since 2000, however, the birthrate has dropped to an average of 1.4 births annually for every 100 women of childbearing age. With Baby Boomers becoming eligible for Social Security in 2008, we will see a disproportionate 3:1 ratio of retirees to job market entries. Immigration growth will alleviate this considerably, but with that comes a new set of challenges, such as an increasing number of limited English proficient students.

These demographic trends are the reason that Social Security and other retirement systems – including pension plans – are in jeopardy of collapse. It is a mathematical certainty that our nation cannot afford to allow these trends to continue without taking preventative action soon. Our nation simply cannot afford to wait and hope for the best any longer, especially with other major challenges on the horizon.

Medicare is another enormous challenge facing us. In 2004, 9 percent of the federal budget was spent on Medicare; in 2020 it will be 25 percent. By 2040, it is projected that 50 percent of the federal budget will be spent on Medicare. Government projections also indicate that by 2040 Medicare and Social Security spending combined will more than wipe out the entire federal budget, with no resources available for schools, national defense, or anything else.

The looming civil rights and economic crises we face are far beyond anything the nation has experienced in the past. These factors helped to convince Senator Edward Kennedy to sponsor NCLB and President George W. Bush to embrace it. We need to understand and accept that NCLB – as a mechanism to ensure that the next generation will be competitive in the world economy – is not just a senseless piece of legislation imposed upon educators, but legislation that is crucial to our nation's security and well-being.

Technology

Another critical factor to consider is technology. Many of us can remember the first mainframe computers, which filled entire rooms, required four technicians to operate them, and were fed data by inserting punch cards. The earliest mainframes had a grand total of eight megabytes of storage capacity. In 1976, the personal computer (PC) first hit the market. The natural progression of technology has armed us with the far more portable laptop computers we enjoy today. Gradually, now the laptop is being replaced by the personal digitized assistant (PDA), which allows us to access e-mail and the Internet from anywhere we travel. These devices have so much more speed and capacity than the early mainframes or even early PCs that we must pause and wonder how we survived such primitive technologies. As technology continues to get smaller, it becomes more and more an extension of our beings.

Moore's Law – an observation and prediction by Intel co-founder Gordon Moore about how quickly the rate of data capacity increases for technology components – quantifies the processing power of a computer chip as doubling every 18 months. Similar principles indicate that biotechnology- and nanotechnology-based information systems will double in processing power every 27 months.

The transformation of technology from PCs to cell phones to PDAs and more is possible thanks to the advancement of nanotechnology. Nanotechnology uses the atom as the fundamental building block for technology development. Nanotech companies are now manufacturing computer chips that are 1/1000 the width of a human hair. These computer chips have as much computing power as traditional silicon chips. Soon we will see a quantum leap in computing capacity as we move toward the total integration of information technology, nanotechnology, and biotechnology. By integrating the various areas of technology, researchers will have the ability to manipulate and develop life systems similar to the way software systems are developed.

Biotechnologies also are developing at an impressive rate. Advancements in biotechnology now make possible a new method of selecting and sorting young people. Knowledge of one's genetic makeup can identify an individual's learning styles and aptitudes, and whether he or she is an inductive or deductive reasoner. Some Asian nations believe that they can use the genetic composition of students to place them in education programs that best suit their DNA. In America, this process would be considered a civil liberties violation if made mandatory. We have a tradition of educational equity, a tradition of providing the opportunity to learn to as broad a cross-section of the population as possible. Limiting students' choices based on genetic criteria would certainly bring a public outcry and would be in direct conflict with such legislation as the Americans with Disabilities Act and NCLB.

As discussed at length earlier in this chapter, China is the world leader in clothes, shoes, and furniture manufacturing. They also lead the world in the production of consumer electronics and computers, meaning that nation has taken over a very significant sector of the technology industry. China is now positioned to become the world leader in the research and development of biotechnology and nanotechnology. They understand the competition they face in America, Europe, India, and the other Pacific Rim nations, but the numbers are in their favor. Some 60 percent of all bachelor's degrees in China are awarded in the areas of science and engineering, which has experts predicting that 90 percent of the world's scientists and engineers will work in Asia by 2010. The fact that it costs five times as much in America to employ a scientist or engineer than it does in China only exacerbates the problem that the United States faces. A highly skilled population willing to work for low wages is a concept that seems foreign to the American value system.

Changing Values and Attitudes

The fourth trend to consider is values and attitudes. Each generation acquires a different set of values and expectations than the ones before it. Neil Howe and William Strauss, respected authors and experts in the field of generation studies, believe that every generation attempts to reverse what it perceives as the worst characteristics of older generations and to fill the roles being vacated by the dying generation. Howe and Strauss contend that this cyclical process – four generations complete a cycle – has been proven over the course of history. If this is true, today's students have very large shoes to fill because history has marked them as successors to the World War II-winning G.I.s, the ones iconic newsman Tom Brokaw labeled the "Greatest Generation."

This Greatest Generation, or G.I. Generation, was born in the first quarter of the 20th century. They experienced the Roaring Twenties and the Great Depression. They fought in World War II. They were great risk-takers and team players. They were responsible, in large part, for the restructuring of America's education, business, and government systems. This generation valued a high school diploma and considered it sufficient for success in life.

The G.I. Generation gave birth to the Silent Generation – labeled as such because they were expected to stay out of the way while their parents were busy fighting the Germans and Japanese. They grew up feeling that they were born too late to do great deeds and felt it was their responsibility to protect the status quo. This generation also placed great value on graduating from high school.

Immediately following World War II and up to the mid-1960s, the Baby Boomers were born. Generally, this generation was deeply into individual needs and was considered self-absorbed. Its members, railing against what they saw as a cultural sterility and sensibility among their parents, failed to see the importance of a high school diploma, though they got one anyway. Some began to see the value of a college education as necessary to success. Baby Boomers were, and continue to be, culture creators, leaving an indelible mark on American society.

Baby Boomers spawned Generation X, or Gen-Xers, a reactive and nomadic lot. The self-absorption of their parents made them feel under-protected as children and felt they had to raise themselves. As a result, Gen-Xers grew up quickly as a generation and were responsible for the dot.com boom of the 1990s. They were pragmatic about the value of a high school diploma and did not view it as sufficient for success.

Howe and Strauss have named the next generation "Millennials." Mostly the children of Gen-Xers, they are the ones filling K-12 classrooms today. The Baby Boomers were content to entrust their children's education to the schools. Gen-Xers do the opposite. They want to be involved in every aspect of their children's education, often to the chagrin of many teachers and the students themselves. They are what Howe and Strauss call "helicopter parents." Their willingness to challenge school policy and the techniques and decisions of teachers has placed additional pressure on the American education system. Interestingly enough, public opinion polls of parents of Millennials show that they generally support a push for new standards and are not nearly as opposed to tough testing requirements as educators are.

Millennials are not like their parents or grandparents, though. In their book, *Millennials Rising – the Next Great Generation*, Howe and Strauss make the point that "millennial attitudes and behaviors represent a sharp break from Generation X, and are running exactly counter to trends launched by the Boomers." They are respectful, civic minded, collaborative, less likely to smoke or drink, and are good students. Both the National Association of Educational Progress (NAEP) and Trends in International Mathematics and Science Study (TIMSS) show a steady increase in student performance, especially among lower grades. Of all the trends discussed to this point, the increasing proficiency of students is by far the most positive.

Millennials are the largest group of young spenders in history, but not much of what they spend is their own money. This generation is growing up in an era of unparalleled affluence and many of their acquisitions – X-Boxes, DVDs and Game Boys – are gifts or co-purchases provided by parents or grandparents. Whereas China, India, and Eastern European countries are committed to establishing a middle class, Millennials have known no other scenario. They likely believe a middle-class lifestyle is a birthright, having never experienced the challenges that faced earlier generations.

The world today is an exciting one. Unfortunately, America is not presently positioned to maintain the level of leadership it enjoyed in the past. Other nations have made great strides in a short period of time of readying themselves for the future. America has been unable to keep pace with the changes going on in the world and is finding it more difficult to compete in the global economy. While the general public may not be aware of these challenges, one sector of the American population that really understands the dynamics of competition at the national and global level is the American business community. The economic trends became evident to them in the early 1980s with the dramatic decline in the number of unskilled jobs. Jobs that were once routine and sequential have been eliminated or replaced by technology that speeds production and reduces costs. Furthermore, the ease with which information can be shared allows businesses to outsource work overseas with a high-quality, low-cost return. Medium wage, high-skill jobs are the standard for today's global economy. Unfortunately, the high cost of American labor, coupled with the vast amount of money required to support an aging population, makes outsourcing very desirable to American companies. There are ways to reverse these trends, and many options begin with educational reform in our schools.

Challenges to Change

As we have discussed, the challenges of a changing economy and society are ever-present. Family life, the workplace, and community are all fundamentally different today than they were even 10 years ago. Education is integral to maintaining society's cultural and structural stability, and much of the responsibility for meeting and overcoming these challenges has been placed on our schools. A "back to basics" rallying cry has ensued, but the skills that high school graduates – and all individuals – need for success in the 21st century's information-based society are vastly different from those needed in the past.

Educational leaders face many obstacles to meet current and future challenges. Education must break free of certain traditions and reign in the standards movement. It must begin to really look at the learning styles of today's generation of students and alter instructional strategies to best meet their needs. Today's students are fundamentally different thinkers and learners than their predecessors. They require a highly rigorous and broad skill set to be work-ready upon graduation. Schools must develop a culture of excellence that challenges every student to acquire the critical thinking skills to achieve rigorous and relevant standards. They must develop relevant curricula to inspire students to excel.

While we often hear the call for rigor and relevance, leaders frequently are adding a third "R" to the mix: *relationships*. They are now calling for schools that aspire to "rigor, relevance, and relationships" to address the increasing recognition about the critically important role relationships play in successful learning. It is impossible to forecast exactly where the future will take us, but it is obvious that, as technology continues to evolve, it also will continue to alter and shape the workplace and our homes, personal lives, and education systems.

What are the challenges to changing our schools? The major obstacles include overcrowded curricula, the skills gap, and outdated school models.

Overcrowded Curricula

When everything is a priority, nothing is a priority. Traditionally, American schools have presented an overabundance of knowledge-driven material to be taught. With so little or no time to effectively plan instruction that is both rigorous and relevant, teachers do not have the opportunity to help students develop the process skills or sense of relevance needed to apply such knowledge to practical situations. These skills are essential for success in postsecondary studies and adult roles.

Traditionally, the reflexive response to teach modern-day skills and knowledge to students has been to stuff the curriculum with more content standards. Nothing is ever taken off the plate, however, and little or no time is allotted for teachers to help students develop the critical-thinking skills that will enable them to engage and apply the standards content in meaningful ways.

The way American schools and American culture are organized have become the biggest obstacles to school reform and higher standards. Offering discrete courses taught in isolation, with little connection to other subjects or other learning, may be compatible with teacher training and certification, but it bears no resemblance to the integrated way knowledge is used in life.

Although high-stakes state assessments and teacher accountability were intended to increase student proficiency, this initiative has backfired on a number of fronts. When schools focus on getting at-risk students to pass tests, so much time is wasted in test preparation that more essential subject matter, those things not tested, is neglected. This is a disservice to students. Although more of them may pass the tests, they are merely becoming test ready rather than workplace ready.

Furthermore, as a society, we have come to view preparing students for college as the primary goal of K-12 schooling. Yet, while the level of skills needed for employment climbs every year, requirements for college entry stay the same or even diminish in years when demographics produce a dip in the number of high school graduates and many colleges struggle to fill seats.

Skills Gaps

The gap between technology and education continues to widen in America because education in this country is not adapting to societal changes. As discussed earlier, recent studies point to the need to provide all students with an academically rigorous and relevant education. Just as the education system designed for the agrarian calendar made little sense in the industrial age, the education system of the industrial age makes no sense in today's information-based society. The growth of Asian and Eastern European competitors threatens to continue widening the gap between the skills our children are acquiring and those they need to succeed in the ever-evolving international marketplace. Rigor and relevance are keys to preparing students for the challenges ahead. Schools need to fix the antiquated systems model if they are serious about getting all students to the high standards necessary for them to excel globally.

System Models: Schools Versus the Real World

The American education system is just that: a system. Improving the system requires changing the inputs or changing the process. Yet, education is unlike any other system in the United States. It is a system with certain constraints that other industry models do not have. The desired output for the education system is work- or college-ready high school graduates who have received a rigorous and relevant education. However, the education system inputs are students, real people who cannot be changed or discarded because the United States is committed to providing *all* children with access to an education.

Schools Versus Students

A school's success is primarily dependent upon student learning, which is influenced by three primary factors:
- what is taught
- students' willingness and ability to learn
- how things are taught

In the quest to raise standards in schools, we, as a nation, have become fixated on what to teach with a focus on what can be assessed. We have not paid enough attention to students' willingness and ability to learn and how we should teach to their learning styles. Yet, these factors are the basis of effective instruction.

Instruction needs to be focused on how students learn. Students today learn differently because they have been "wired" differently. The ubiquitous technological environment in which they have grown up and engaged in for their entire lives has had a profound impact on the way they think, learn, and interact. How successful a school is in teaching today's students depends on a clear understanding of how youth learn from early childhood through adolescence.

In recent years, research about how the brain develops has grown significantly. Through MRI advancements, for example, scientists have discovered a massive proliferation of gray matter in children between the ages 6 to 12. During this time, children develop enormous brain capacity to learn in many areas. It is also a time when children transition from being highly skilled dependant learners to novice independent thinkers. The proliferation of gray matter is followed by a pruning period that lasts for several years. Pruning, also known as the "use-it-or-lose-it" phase, is a time when neurons that are frequently stimulated make connections with other neurons, allowing for growth, while neurons that are idle wither and die.

Technology and science have provided educators with a map of the adolescent brain and an explanation of how this complex organ works. This knowledge can empower teachers to make curricular and instructional decisions that have effective impacts on learning. It also challenges them to provide stimulating instruction and activities that will foster learning for every student in class. To meet these challenges, educators must:

- provide flexible and safe environments that encourage students to challenge themselves without the fear of failure
- develop rigorous and relevant curricula and use instructional techniques designed to meet students' varying abilities
- involve students in the collaborative establishment of classroom rules and procedures
- encourage exploration of creative alternative solutions to school and classroom tasks
- thoroughly explain the complex development and function of the brain so students can understand the biology behind their own learning process, including many of the major obstacles and challenges they are facing
- foster a supportive environment that will allow for trial and error

- use multiple assessments – such as portfolios, rubrics, teacher observation, and student performance – to gauge student success and academic development
- encourage and allow for children to develop individually and at their own paces
- use cooperative learning and activities that stimulate positive student emotion, such as debates and real-world experiences
- understand that state assessments are a starting point, not a finish line.

Solutions for Meaningful School Reform

Throughout the United States, many schools are working diligently to improve education practices. At the heart of these improvement efforts lies a strong commitment to meet the needs of learners, to raise scores on standardized tests in all academic areas, and to satisfy the mandates embedded in NCLB. It is frustrating, however, if schools embrace this goal without a systematic approach for measuring student learning, setting goals, monitoring progress, and recognizing successes.

Some school improvement initiatives are carefully constructed, viewed appropriately through the lens of a school's mission, driven by data, and accountable to multiple stakeholders. Other initiatives, however, are not so meticulously conceived. Rather than allowing data to drive goal setting and decision making, some schools are still guided by good intentions, hunches, and impressions. Often, these schools inadvertently lose sight of learners' needs as they struggle to ensure compliance with state and federal regulations.

Striving for Success

The process of improving student performance comes in many different forms and packages. It may be referred to as school improvement, school reform, or school restructuring. But no matter what it's called, ultimately it comes down to a single goal: raising student achievement through a rigorous and relevant education.

Since founding the International Center for Leadership in Education, my colleagues and I have partnered with thousands of schools and school districts across the county to work on sustainable, whole school reform issues. In working with these schools and districts as they have made concerted efforts at reform, we have identified two overarching characteristics about the process to be true:

- change needs to be evolutionary and not revolutionary
- each school community has its own proverbial DNA, so what works in one does not necessarily translate to another

Further, as we looked closely at high performing schools, we found that they each abided by the some basic principles, or components, which are the basis of the chapters of this book. These components were identified, defined, and refined, and now they are the basis of the Learning Criteria to Support 21st Century Learners.™ The Learning Criteria, presented in greater detail in Chapter 2, is a valuable tool that offers a guideline for translating beliefs and vision into actions through goal-setting and measuring benchmarks. In essence, the Learning Criteria helps schools measure "success beyond the test" and supports creation of a culture that understands that state testing and AYP are essential, but not adequate in meeting the needs of all learners. When a school uses the Learning Criteria to guide the improvement process, they follow a clearly outlined course of information collection and analysis. The result is a plan that helps schools recognize where they are, determine where they want to go, and chart a successful course for achieving improvement.

Component #1: Embrace a Common Vision and Goals – Rigor, Relevance, and Relationships for *All* Students

The key to any school improvement initiative is the development of a shared vision that establishes and maintains awareness of the need for change. Change will not occur in schools unless teachers, parents, students, and the general public understand that continuous improvement is needed.

Schools must communicate their message to the community during back-to-school nights, community newsletters, meetings with parents, community forums, etc. In addition, educators have to believe that all students can learn. Teachers must recognize that a wide variety of delivery and support systems must be put in place to enable students to achieve their potential and achieve high standards.

In the end, the goal is to create more pressure for change than resistance to change. Some of the intended outcomes of this component are:

- Leaders of the process, staff, students, and stakeholders can articulate the reasons for change and can describe the vision of school improvement.
- Through processes, structures, attitudes, and actions, leadership and staff exhibit a change culture of high expectations that embraces rigor, relevance, and relationships for *all* students.
- Staff and stakeholders take ownership of an improvement plan that features clear goals and objectives.
- Leadership is focused on sustaining momentum for change and on reducing resistance to it.

Component #2: Inform Decisions Through Data Systems

Whole school or district reform is an ongoing event guided by a well-developed data structure that is based on multiple measures of student learning. Highly successful schools and districts understand this process and use current data to make decisions about curriculum, instruction, and assessment. Using data, they accurately validate areas of strengths and needs, identify priority issues, and effectively make adjustments in order to meet the needs of all students. They share key data appropriately with stakeholders. When executed well, these coordinated efforts result in:

- measurable learning goals and criteria that are based on defined education values and a vision shared by leadership and staff

- strategic planning that is tied to data-driven decision making, with day-to-day activities that are connected with overarching goals
- decision making, goal setting, and progress measurement that are grounded in current data
- school success being based on multiple measures of student achievement using the Learning Criteria's four areas: (1) core academic learning, (2) stretch learning, (3) learner engagement, and (4) personal skill development

Component #3: Empower Leadership Teams to Take Action and Innovate

Successful schools and districts are led by individuals who possess and communicate a vision of learning that will equip graduates with the skills to compete in a global, high-tech, and competitive world. Yet, school and district administrators must lead systems and institutions that are inherently resistant to change. Leaders in the highest performing districts and schools cultivate relationships; build broad-based momentum for school improvement efforts; and create a shared vision regarding what to change and how to change it. Meaningful, sustained reform is facilitated when leadership guides teachers, staff, parents, and community stakeholders to embrace a shared vision of school improvement. Success is achieved when:

- The effectiveness of school and district leadership is apparent to all.
- Leadership is distributed among staff that is knowledgeable of change management principles and processes.
- Current leaders are retained and energized, and new, prospective leadership talent is identified and developed.
- Capacity and momentum maintain the vision of continuous improvement and sustain a culture of rigor, relevance, and relationships.

Component #4: Clarify Student Learning Expectations

In most schools and districts, the curriculum is bloated. It has expanded to the point of being unwieldy in scope and breadth. As a consequence, district and school leadership, along with staff, need to be aware of and understand their state standards, as well as how their curriculum maps to them. They must have access to reliable assessment data so that they can review state test blueprints, determine which standards are truly priorities, and set curriculum priorities throughout the district.

Successful districts and schools recognize that state standards and assessments must be viewed as minimum requirements for all students; students need additional skills and knowledge for success after graduation. Successful districts and schools have implemented coherent, prioritized curricula with mutually reinforcing components that address what students need to know and be able to do to be successful in life and what knowledge they need to be successful on high-stakes tests.

How does this look in a successful school? First, the school culture and focus clearly emphasize standards. Second, curricula are clearly articulated, scaffolded, and prioritized by subject and are aligned to state, local, and industry standards. Finally, learning expectations and student proficiency levels are clearly defined with:

- prioritized, locally developed skills and knowledge outcomes, curriculum maps, and assessments
- crosswalks among academic subjects, arts education, career and technical education
- district and school instructional improvement plans
- teacher instructional plans

Component #5: Adopt Effective Instructional Practices

Helping individual students to attain the highest appropriate levels of academic rigor should be the goal of all educators. This notion needs to be balanced with the recognition that relevance makes rigor possible, but only when trusting and respectful relationships among students, teachers, staff, and students are embedded in instruction. Relationships nurture both rigor and relevance.

Effective instruction must be adjusted to serve the needs of individual learners; be based on the high expectations set by a caring teacher; and informed by brain-based research. Successful instructional practices integrate reading and writing strategies, including document, technological, and quantitative literacy strategies, and are differentiated and adapted to meet the needs of diverse classrooms that include students with disabilities, students whose primary language is not English, and students who are disengaged. When effective instructional practices are truly in place:

- Teachers are conversant with the Rigor/Relevance Framework and design instruction accordingly.
- Differentiated and personalized instruction built on positive relationships is evident in all classrooms.
- Instructional needs of special education students, English language learners, and disengaged students are accommodated.
- All teachers address literacy and mathematical proficiency, and they personalize learning.

Component #6: Address Organizational Structures

Organizational structure should be determined by instructional needs. A "begin with the end in mind" approach allows highly successful schools to see clearly the organizational structures that need to be changed in order to support and engage all students. Many schools mistakenly adopt a new organization without clearly understanding what will be different instructionally as a result of the change. In successful schools, organizational structure is used as a tool or resource to support instruction and engagement and to help prepare all students for the demands of the 21st century.

By focusing first on effective instructional strategies and practices, highly successful schools design safe, secure, and caring learning environments that enhance relationships and personalize instruction for all students through such structures as small learning communities; career and technical education; supportive transitional programs; and community partnerships that provide work-based experiences and meaningful internships. Such structures facilitate staff collaboration, connect students with caring adults, and nurture learning environments designed to provide students with rigorous coursework, relevant experiences, and meaningful relationships with teachers who will help them attain their goals and aspirations. In a successful school:

- The school is results-driven and focused on effective instruction.
- Programs, structures, and the physical environment are designed to reinforce relationships, address student needs, and offer a safe, secure, nurturing, and engaging environment for learning.
- Instructional goals determine organizational issues and structures; organizational issues and structures are adapted to support the learning needs of all students, to forge staff collaboration, and to provide a personalized environment that supports relationships and encourages achievement.
- Time, use of space, "environmentals," physical plant, and resources are aligned with student learning and engagement goals.

Component #7: Monitor Student Progress/Improve Support Systems

Although many ongoing school processes and practices were originally devised to classify students by ability group, today's education leaders are challenged with providing meaningful learning experiences for *all* students. Educators need to ensure that all students graduate from high school as college-, career-, and life-ready young adults. To accomplish this goal, student progress and attainment need to be constantly measured with the resulting data being used to help each student achieve proficiency.

Because students arrive at school at various points along the academic achievement and needs spectrum, schools must provide meaningful support systems that identify, and then help close, gaps in student learning. Effective support systems need to be built upon strong relationships that nurture student achievement. Finally, highly successful programs recognize the need to monitor student progress on a regular basis. They recognize the necessity of state testing, but view the data as informative, not sufficient, to have an optimal impact on student performance. Successful schools also use formative assessments in an organized, deliberate, and ongoing fashion to monitor student progress; they then use the data to adjust instructional practices as needed. Ultimately, when a school is truly successful in its improvement efforts:

- Achievement, learning, engagement, and progress data are monitored and analyzed regularly for all students.
- Students with special needs are identified and provided with services to drive success in learning and achievement.
- Multiple pathways to achievement are offered.
- Academic intervention strategies are available; are understood by staff, students, and stakeholders; and are used fully and effectively.

Component #8: Refine Process on an Ongoing Basis

Success is an ongoing process. Student needs, community demographics, state requirements, and college- and work-ready skills are continually changing. Successful schools use a planning process that continuously monitors and considers student learning and performance, examines ongoing and emerging challenges, and explores potential solutions and successful practices from around the country. At a successful school:

- Goals are based on the Learning Criteria and are monitored and frequently measured against the school improvement plan.
- The system includes continuous review and refinement of the school improvement process as well as a commitment to monitoring national trends, local needs, successful models, and best practices.

CHAPTER TWO

Begin With the End in Mind:

Inform Decisions Through Data Systems

C an American schools teach everything that every advocate wants them to teach? The 1960s and the 1970s were decades in which the roles and responsibilities placed on schools across the nation kept expanding. That brought an explosion in what we expected teachers to cover in their curricula. When I was head of the division for curriculum and instruction for the New York State Education Department in the 1980s, the state, like many others, was attempting to bring focus to a curriculum crowded with outdated material. But in our efforts to focus the curriculum, we fell prey to the very same problems as the educators of the preceding decades: instead of trimming the curriculum by pruning obsolete material, we added more content. And, as various special interest groups came to the table to make their cases, the curriculum ballooned.

Then came the *No Child Left Behind Act of 2001* (NCLB), with the requirement for every state to develop standards and testing programs. As states worked diligently to develop their standards, everyone seemed to agree that enough was enough.

It was time to bring focus and cohesiveness to the curriculum by retaining essential content and eliminating the things that were just "nice to know." In the first decade of the 21st century, however, we have failed again. We have not trimmed the fat; instead we have again expanded atop existing content.

As we collectively consider schools today, it is clear that we have classroom teachers on a treadmill. They have been charged with covering more material than they actually have time to cover, so what ends up being taught is what is on the test. But is this the best we have to offer our students? I don't think so. To address this issues, the International Center has developed a tool – the Rigor/Relevance Framework – for examining curriculum, instruction, and assessment.

Rigor/Relevance Framework™

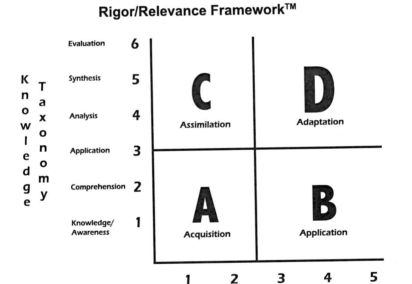

Application Model

Start With Rigor and Relevance

Since my colleagues and I began using the Rigor/Relevance Framework in presentations and discussions around the country, it has gained in popularity as a clear yet comprehensive, descriptive way to understand what schools need to do to prepare students for the future. The framework consists of two continuums, the Knowledge Taxonomy and the Application Model, along with four quadrants – Acquisition, Application, Assimilation, and Adaptation – representing knowledge types.

The Knowledge Taxonomy describes the increasingly complex ways in which we think. It is based on the six levels of Bloom's Taxonomy:

1. knowledge
2. comprehension
3. application
4. analysis
5. synthesis
6. evaluation

The low end of this continuum involves acquiring knowledge and being able to recall or locate that knowledge in a simple manner. Just as a computer completes a word search in a word processing program, a competent person at this level can scan through thousands of bits of information in the brain to locate that desired knowledge.

The high end of the Knowledge Taxonomy labels more complex ways in which individuals use knowledge. At this level, knowledge is fully integrated into one's mind, and individuals can do much more than locate information. They can take several pieces of knowledge and combine them in both logical and creative ways. Assimilation (Quadrant C) of knowledge is a good way to describe this high level of the thinking continuum. Assimilation is often referred to as a higher-order thinking skill; at this level, the student can solve multi-step problems and create unique work and solutions.

The second continuum, the Application Model, is one of action. While the low end of the continuum is knowledge acquired for its own sake, the high end signifies action. Knowledge at the high end of the continuum is used to solve complex real-world problems and to create projects, designs, and other works for use in real-life situations. The Application Model measures the knowledge to action continuum across five levels:

1. knowledge in one discipline
2. application of knowledge in one discipline
3. application of knowledge across disciplines
4. application of knowledge to solve real-world, predictable problems or situations
5. application of knowledge to solve real-world, unpredictable problems or situations

In addition to the Knowledge Taxonomy and the Application Model continuums, the framework is divided into four quadrants, each of which is labeled with a term that characterizes the learning or student performance at that level.

Quadrant A: Acquisition

Quadrant A represents simple recall and basic understanding of knowledge for its own sake. Students gather and store bits of knowledge and information and are primarily expected to remember or understand this acquired knowledge. Knowing that the world is round or that Shakespeare wrote *Hamlet* are examples of Quadrant A knowledge.

Quadrant B: Application

Quadrant B represents action or a high degree of application for knowledge. Students use acquired knowledge to solve problems, design solutions, and complete work. The highest level of application is to apply appropriate knowledge to new and unpredictable situations. Knowing how to use math skills to make purchases and count change are two examples.

Quadrant C: Assimilation

Quadrant C represents more complex thinking than that of Quadrant A, but is still knowledge for its own sake. Students extend and refine their acquired knowledge to be able to use

44

that knowledge automatically and routinely to analyze and solve problems and create unique solutions. Thus, Quadrant C embraces higher levels of knowledge, such as knowing how the U.S. political system works and analyzing the benefits and challenges of the cultural diversity of this nation versus other nations.

Quadrant D: Adaptation

Quadrant D, like Quadrant B, represents action or a high degree of application. Students have the competence to think in complex ways and also to apply the knowledge and skills they have acquired. Even when confronted with perplexing unknowns, students are able to use extensive knowledge and skills to create solutions and take actions that further develop their skills and knowledge. The ability to access information in wide-area network systems and the ability to gather knowledge from a variety of sources to solve a complex problem in the workplace are types of Quadrant D knowledge.

Using the Rigor/Relevance Framework as a reference, we can now easily see that the most useful preparation for students is Quadrant D: Adaptation, while the most testable is Quadrant A: Acquisition. Yet, we find schools typically teaching students – especially at the high school level – in the B or C quadrants. Quadrant C may represent the college prep program with strong academics, but that often shows little relevance to the curriculum. Quadrant B may represent career and technical education, which has basic knowledge with a lot of real-world application but not especially sophisticated content. Thus, we have taken an interesting position here early in the new millennium. We knew prior to NCLB that we needed to raise standards in a curriculum that was often based on quadrants B and C. But in our attempt to raise standards to prepare students for Quadrant D, we have actually driven many schools back toward Quadrant A.

High performing schools recognize that this is foolhardy. They have done what states have attempted but failed to do with their standards. They have separated what is essential from what is nice to know. They have made the hard calls by recognizing that everything in a curriculum is not of equal value.

As they have done that, they have also raised another central question for themselves: "What is the purpose of K-12 education?" Is the purpose of K-12 education to instill knowledge in students? Is the purpose to teach students how to apply knowledge that they will need to know in the 21st century? Should the focus be on developing personal competence, such as perseverance, cooperation, and organizational skills? Or is it something else?

Supporting 21st Century Learners:
The Learning Criteria

In Chapter 1, we discussed at length the challenges that a changing economy and society pose for our nation. Family life, the workplace, and community are all fundamentally different today than they were even 10 years ago. Because education is integral to maintaining society's cultural and structural stability, much of the responsibility for meeting and overcoming these challenges has been placed on our schools. A "back to basics" rallying cry has ensued, but the skills that high school graduates – and all individuals – need for success in the 21st century information-based society are vastly different from those needed in the past. Unfortunately, the gap between the skills that curricula provide, and that society in general and the workplace in particular need, continues to deepen. Much of today's K-12 curriculum is still set up to support what is now an obsolete industrial era. We need to catch up.

Yet the need for change faces resistance on a number of fronts. School curricula are overcrowded: when we try to make everything our number one priority, we end up with no priorities. The rapid pace of globalization is accelerating the gap between the skills Americans have and the skills they will need to succeed in the future. Brain research indicates that the way our students are taught is sometimes at odds with the way they actually learn. Yet, though the need for educational changes grows by the day, the American education system itself is a model that resists change.

The International Center's Learning Criteria to Support 21st Century Learners™ is one tool that supports school improvement processes through a step-by-step collection and analysis process. In the hands of a thoughtful, broad-based school leadership team, the Learning Criteria framework helps schools clarify their missions, prioritize problems and interventions, and critically review school performance. Further, these analyses provide critical rationales for establishing goals and developing action plans. Most importantly, the data generated by the Learning Criteria reflects the needs of learners in ways that less complex and more traditional measures overlook. The framework is designed to provide a robust, comprehensive, and detailed portrait of school performance that clearly maps out a route for school improvement efforts.

Increased expectations and testing demands have placed a heavy burden on schools. The Learning Criteria accounts for both expectations and demands. Simultaneously, it breaks new ground in the territory of school improvement in that it redefines school success in terms of what is unique to each school, in terms that meet standardized test measures of school success, and in terms that reveal the school environment in all of its complexity and depth.

Every community and every school has its own DNA, which means that what is true for one school may not be appropriate for the next. But don't forget: the majority of what kids need to know and be able to do does not change from one school to the next.

High performing schools have developed comprehensive learning criteria for their schools. They have held the line on "less is more." They are attuned to the fact that the purpose of public education goes beyond what can simply be measured on a test. They *do* do a great job of preparing kids for the test; in fact, they see that as essential, though not adequate.

The Learning Criteria is arranged in four data categories – Core Academic Learning, Stretch Learning, Learner Engagement, and Personal Skill Development – that educators can use to determine the success of their school in preparing students for current assessments as well as for future roles and responsibilities. School leaders must be very deliberate in assembling their learning criteria so that their school improvement plans balance the school's unique qualities with what we know and understand are the necessary elements of success for any school. A school should have data indicators in each of the four categories listed, with at least one indicator in each category applying to the school's entire student population.

Core Academic Learning

Core academic learning refers to achievement in the core subjects of English language arts, mathematics, science, and other subjects identified by the school. Sample data indicators include:

- percentage of students meeting proficiency levels on state tests (required)
- average scores on ACT/SAT/PSAT tests
- achievement levels on standardized tests other than state exams
- percentage of students requiring English language arts or mathematics remediation in college
- follow-up surveys of graduates' academic achievements
- percentage of students graduating high school in four years
- percentage of students earning a college degree within four years after high school completion
- military ASVAB score

The International Center believes that core academic learning and state testing are essential, but not adequate. They are the beginning of what students need to know and be able to do – not the finish line as so many have made them – and they predominantly represents Quadrant A learning on the Rigor/Relevance Framework.

Stretch Learning

Stretch learning is the demonstration of rigorous and relevant learning beyond minimum requirements through participation and achievement in higher level learning or specialized courses. Sample data indicators include:

- number of credits required to graduate
- average number of credits earned at graduation
- interdisciplinary work and projects, such as a senior exhibition
- participation/test scores in International Baccalaureate courses
- average number of college credits earned by high school graduation through dual enrollment
- enrollment in advanced mathematics or science courses
- enrollment in Advanced Placement (AP) courses, scores on AP exams, and percentage of participants achieving a score of 3 or higher on a five-point scale
- percentage of students completing career majors or career/technical education programs
- four or more credits in a career area
- four or more credits in arts
- three or more years of foreign language
- value of scholarships earned at graduation
- achievement of specialized certificates (e.g., Microsoft, Cisco Academy)

Stretch learning is difficult because it compels schools to define how they are stimulating and stretching each and every student, not just the best and brightest. If schools are truly stretching them, students will spend most of their time in quadrants C and D of the Rigor/Relevance Framework.

Learner Engagement

Student engagement is the extent to which students (1) are motivated and committed to learning, (2) have a sense of belonging and accomplishment, and (3) have relationships with adults, peers, and parents who support learning. Sample data indicators include:

- student satisfaction surveys
- student risk behaviors
- dropout rate
- attendance rate
- graduation rate

- tardiness rate
- discipline referrals
- participation rates in extracurricular activities
- follow-up surveys about enrollment in higher education
- percentage of students taking ACT or SAT
- surveys about the degree to which teachers know their students
- surveys about positive peer relationships
- percentage of students going to two-year colleges
- percentage of students going to four-year colleges

Students need to be engaged before they can apply higher order, creative thinking skills. They learn most effectively when the teacher and the material being taught make sense. This can only happen if the teacher has created a safe learning environment that encourages students to meet challenges and apply high-rigor skills to real-world, unpredictable situations inside and outside of school.

Personal Skill Development

Personal skill development includes (1) measures of personal, social, service, and leadership skills and (2) demonstrations of positive behaviors and attitudes. Respect, responsibility, and perseverance are examples of skills or attributes that are included in this category. Sample data indicators include:

- percentage of students participating in service-learning opportunities
- presence of students in leadership positions for clubs or sports
- assessment of personal skills, such as time management, ability to plan and organize work, leadership, being a team player, etc.
- respect for diversity
- opportunities for and evidence of teamwork
- character traits, such as trustworthiness, perseverance, etc.
- conflict resolution processes in place
- reduction in number of student incidences of conflict

- results of follow-up surveys of graduates about development of personal skills

Consider a son or daughter's new friend. Are you more concerned about the friend's grades or about his or her character qualities? Personal skill development gets to the heart of what makes a citizen, friend, or community member an effective worker. What are schools doing to promote these qualities? Are they making leadership opportunities available for all students? Are they creating a curriculum that teaches these skills and making them graduation requirements?

If a school effectively addresses personal skill development and student engagement, then core learning and stretch learning become exceedingly easier to address. A focus on just core learning or on just a combination of core and stretch learning may lead to marginal success in those criteria, but it will not allow a school to achieve true overall success. Unfortunately, that is what many schools in the country are doing because this approach may appear to help student achievement by raising test scores. For real success, however, schools need to address all four criteria. By doing so, they are helping shape well-rounded students who have the skills to succeed in the 21st century.

Stepping Up: Using the Learning Criteria for Continuous School Improvement

Using the Learning Criteria to measure success can help a school become more mission driven and goal focused. Schools that have worked with the Learning Criteria report that identifying data indicators has helped them specify what they believe is their school's true purpose and identify what the school and community want students to know and be able to do in many aspects of life. State testing requirements are viewed as one necessary component of this process, not the driving force behind it.

When we talk about "learning criteria," we mean the Learning Criteria to Support 21st Century Learners and the process of using this tool. A school can use the Learning Criteria to build consensus and create a sense of ownership among the stakeholders. Ownership underscores a shared vision, local accountability, and control. Using the Learning Criteria, schools develop their own specific *learning criteria*, with a primary goal of enhancing improvement planning using better data indicators; developing learning criteria is not the same as developing a new improvement process. Thus, the steps for using the Learning Criteria are intended to drive continuous school improvement. While the process individual schools use can vary, this suggested process includes components and tools that many schools have used to effectively and efficiently improve student results.

Step 1: Selection of a Leadership/Data Team

Selection of the leadership/data team is the most important step in the process. When selecting team members, schools must make sure that all school interest groups are represented, including members of the administration, board of education, teachers' association, parent/teacher associations, student government, and the community. This team should consist of seven to 10 members. In subsequent years, team members should be selected by the groups they represent. Once established, the leadership/data team must:

- conduct a thorough review of the school's mission or vision statement
- ensure that the mission or vision statement reflects high expectations for *all* students and the need for continuous improvement
- understand completely the purpose of engaging with the Learning Criteria
- take full ownership over the development of the school's Learning Criteria
- understand its role and responsibilities in promoting school improvement

When each member is committed to progress, focused on school improvement, and fully invested in the Learning Criteria process, the team is ready to move forward. Each member of the leadership/data team must posses a strong working knowledge of the four categories of the Learning Criteria. The team must work together to gather information.

Step 2: Data Collection and Analysis

The leadership/data team must identify what data is currently available, what data is needed, and desired results for each data indicator selected. To accomplish this step, the team must:

- assign roles and responsibilities for collecting necessary data
- create maps to assist in the collection process
- identify key personnel to help in the process
- examine the data, once it is collected, to determine whether it is sustained, disaggregated, and benchmarked

Step 3: Development of School Improvement Goals

Next, the leadership/data team should identify gaps and areas of need in each category. The team will determine at least one area of need from each category, and write a goal statement that is:

- data-driven
- quantitative or qualitative
- meaningful and supportive of the school's mission or vision statement

The completed goal statement identifies strategies that will positively affect learners. With the goals in mind, the team can move to the next step.

Step 4: Development of an Action Plan

Using the goal statement, the leadership/data team can work to develop an action plan to achieve the goals. The plan should provide a step-by step approach including:

- identification of a specific person or group of people responsible for completing each step
- a timeline for when each action step is to be completed

Step 5: Alignment of Goals

The leadership/data team may also use the data and goals

of the learning criteria to align the school with state and federal requirements for comprehensive school improvement.

Step 6: Sharing the School Improvement Plan

It is vital to create a feeling of ownership for the plan within the school and in the community, so when it comes time to present the action plan it is critical to:

- share the school improvement plan with the faculty, staff, administration, board of education, parents, students, and community groups
- establish a system that allows for the collection of feedback and input from all groups
- establish a system that allows for periodic review (e.g., monthly, quarterly, etc.) of the school improvement plan

When the school improvement plan is reviewed and accepted by school and community groups, the team is ready to move into implementation.

Step 7: Evaluation of Progress for Continuous School Improvement

The final step in the process is evaluating the success of the plans implemented. The leadership/data team will determine whether the goals have been achieved and will evaluate the effectiveness of the school improvement plan. Results will be shared with the school community. Effective evaluation of the school improvement plan will:

- identify the need for professional workshops
- identify the need for professional development opportunities
- result in the selection of leadership/data team members for the following year
- show how to begin the process again and again to create a continuous loop

Wanted: Essential Skills

The question of what students need to know to succeed in the 21st century is a complicated one to answer. But we must address it if schools are to educate students successfully and transition them smoothly into life beyond the classroom.

To work toward an answer, the International Center deployed its first essential skills survey, the National Essential Skills Study (NESS), in 1998 and its second one in 2007. The NESS asked educators and the public to identify the essential skills students need in the core areas of English, mathematics, science, and social studies. Essential skills are ones that all students should master in order to be successful after they graduate from high school and move forward into postsecondary studies, careers, and other aspects of life as productive adults and citizens.

The data collected through the surveys is used in the International Center's Curriculum Matrix (see Chapter 4), which identifies each state's most tested standards and performance indicators in its assessment program and also crosswalks the standards to the essential skills. This information can help schools determine where to place emphasis in instruction. At the district and state levels, it can help to establish relevant curricula. For instance, through the Curriculum Matrix, we have found that, depending on the grade level and discipline, typically 20 percent to 40 percent of the benchmarks, performance indicators, or objectives are not tested. Further, the research showed that spending time on the remaining 60 percent to 80 percent leads to improved student performance in those areas.

Three perspectives define curriculum and instruction:
1. What does society expect of students to be successful in the 21st century?
2. What have we learned from brain research about the ways student learn best?
3. How do students view learning?

Merely creating this rich curriculum resource will not be enough, however. It will only be effective in raising student achievement if school staff possess a passion for change that is guided by leadership, driven by data, and supported by continual learning. Since there is not a single standard teaching prescription that will work with every student and in every teaching situation, a curriculum model must include these three perspectives and be flexible enough to consider the complex needs of students. We need to provide teachers with guidelines for rigorous and relevant curricula; data about priority and achievement; and an abundance of curriculum and instructional ideas.

Literacy is Key

Consider literacy. Literacy is a key concern for school systems. Valued employees in the 21st century must be highly literate as well as creative problem-solvers and adaptive to change. They must interact fluidly with ever-changing technology, communicate, and collaborate. But it is a challenge for schools to define exactly what "literacy" means. The business community has long identified inadequate reading proficiency as a leading problem among entry-level employees. Educators have attempted to solve the problem by assigning more reading, mostly literature. But that approach does not bring real-life solutions. The modern definition of literacy needs to encompass far more than just prose. A broad understanding of and familiarity with prose is nice, and that is where most schools focus instruction, but it is not what the future's employees will need in the workplace.

The International Center has researched the level of real-world reading demands using the Lexile Framework® for Reading, developed by MetaMetrics. Lexile measures, as components of an incremental Lexile scale, describe both text difficulty and reader ability, enabling readers to be matched with books that are appropriately engaging and challenging. This innovative approach to reading comprehension, which is discussed in greater depth in Chapter 4, is being widely adopted and implemented in schools across the United States.

Given this discussion, it is hardly surprising that research using the framework indicates that a wide gap exists between the materials used in high school classrooms and those of first-year college literature and textbooks. There is also a gap between reading materials used in high schools and those found in students' communities, including job applications, tax forms, and loan applications. But the widest gap is between high school exit standards in reading and the reading that entry-level employees must do on the job. States need to be sure that the reading proficiency levels they set under NCLB account not just for traditional academic measures of reading competence, but also the skills that will make individuals employable and poise them for success in their lives after graduation.

Remember what we learned from the Curriculum Matrix about relevant curricula? Twenty to 40 percent of standards/benchmarks in a subject might be described as things that are merely nice to know. When schools and districts set forth to create relevant curricula, they need to understand what is vital for student success and develop a flexible model that is infused with instructional strategies to address these essential skills.

Continuing with literacy as an example, we know that employees in most occupations regularly handle forms of text and writing that enable them to complete work, communicate, handle tasks safely, acquire information and goods, establish relationships, and collaborate. Therefore, rather than simply needing increased instruction in traditional literature, students need to be exposed to high levels of document, technological, and quantitative (DTQ) literature so they may develop better reading skills for understanding these kinds of materials (see Chapter 4).

Taking Action

Modifying the curriculum is a promising start, but translating the changes into action is the challenging next step. But there are effective strategies for addressing the instructional side of the question:

Teach and Learn with Rigor and Relevance

As discussed earlier in this chapter, the Rigor/Relevance Framework is an easy-to-understand tool that educators can use when thinking and talking about curriculum and instruction. Recognizing where the concept or skill to be taught fits on the

Rigor/Relevance continuum allows educators to match learning with the instructional process. Thus, the framework helps educators tackle critical questions, such as:

- Is the topic or lesson to be learned academically complex, but not readily applicable in real-world learning situations? Can it be adapted for relevance?
- Is the learning outcome easily applied but not complex on the knowledge hierarchy? Can it be enriched to add rigor to the application?
- How many standards and outcomes within the intended curriculum are clearly within Quadrant A: Acquisition (i.e., that is low academic rigor and low application)?
- How many topics require learning in Quadrant D: Adaptation (i.e., high academic rigor, high level of problem solving application)?
- Does the teaching staff strive to move more and more instruction into Quadrant D, where cognition and engagement are maximized?

Develop a Literacy Plan

The literacy demands of lifelong learning and work after high school are expanding. Yet, far too many secondary level students struggle with class work and state tests. This is not because the subject matter or tasks are too complex, it is because the students have not developed sufficiently high levels of proficiency in reading and literacy. Most reading instruction ends after the elementary grades, and few middle schools or high schools offer dedicated reading instruction. Many schools that are working toward improvement discover that one of the best investments they can make in instruction is the implementation of a schoolwide literacy and reading plan that cover all grades.

Use Data-based Decision Making

These days, most curricula labor under the very weight of themselves. There is simply too much to teach and too much to learn. To alleviate this, something must be taken off the proverbial plate. Education leaders need tools and support to help set priorities in curriculum and instruction. Curriculum Matrix data (see Chapter 4) has helped many individual schools and districts answer the question, "What should I teach?"

Focus on Instruction

Great teachers supported by innovative leaders make the difference. The International Center has worked with thousands of educators to help them to successfully implement strategies that promote "D-Quadrant Instruction" and make high-quality instructional practices central to the entire school's learning culture.

Change or Enhance the Culture of the School

Every school has its own institutional DNA, and some schools are more successful than others. A school's culture and learning environment matter. Do students feel safe, respected, and cared about? Do adults model desired behaviors? Do staff members and students feel that school is a good place to be? Is every student engaged and able to achieve to his or her fullest potential? Is the school a true community of learners? Does the school refuse to accept failure as an option for any student? Leaders need to engineer sustainable culture change and create and sustain a winning attitude among staff, students, and stakeholders. By doing so, they move the school closer to success.

CHAPTER THREE

Team Efforts:
Empower Leadership Teams to Take Action and Innovate

Successful schools can be built, but they cannot be sustained simply through the leadership of just one individual, or even a few individuals.

To sustain successful school reform you need to create leadership teams that include individuals from multiple levels of the organization, including central administration, building-level administrators, classroom teachers, parents, students, and community leaders. They must work as a team together to encourage and support not just the school reform effort itself, but each other as they encounter people or groups that fight change or as unforeseen bumps in the road add new challenges.

Media and various national recognition programs perpetuate the perception that school reform can occur through the heroic and charismatic leadership of a single individual. In my experience, while a single person may be integral to positive results that may occur, this type of leadership structure is not sustainable. There are too many issues, people to address, and areas of expertise needed for one individual, alone, to truly pull off school reform. Furthermore, if reform is built on the back of a single, charismatic leader, as soon as he or she leaves, the reform initiative quickly falls apart.

A really good leader recognizes the need to work with a really good leadership team. A leadership team must begin its work by recognizing that what happens at the classroom level is most critical for student success. Often we get into great debates about organizational structures, physical buildings, school calendars, and bell schedules too early in the reform discussions. My experience shows that having a leadership team address instructional issues at the classroom level *first* is, by far, the most critical element of school reform. Once we deal with instruction, the organizational issues follow.

A Model for Leadership

The process of improving student performance goes by many names, including school improvement, school reform, school reinvention, and school restructuring, among others. No matter what it is called, the ultimate goal is the same: raising student achievement through change.

The actions of school leaders will determine the fate of public education in the 21st century. Maintaining the status quo is not an option. Everyone is seeking change in schools. While all educators must play key roles in changing schools, those in leadership positions bear an even greater burden. They must respond to change appropriately, and they must show others the way.

Change in schools is dynamic. There is no detailed recipe to follow, no single solution for improving our schools. The International Center has worked with schools across the country to identify models, share best practices, and support school leaders in facilitating changes that lead to improvement. Our work reveals that schools typically need to progress through and understand three consecutive stages in order to achieve high academic standards for all students:

- *Why* involves convincing educators, parents, and community members about the reasons a school must change.

- *What* involves the content of change through a common focus by using data, research, and best practices to determine factors need to be addressed for change to come about.
- *How* is determining the process to implement change at the school once people understand and embrace the *why* and the *what*.

Too many schools begin their improvement efforts in the reverse order. They decide how to do things differently before they truly articulate the need or problem. This type of a solution is generally worthless since the problem has not been acknowledged or clarified.

The nature of change is that it must be specific to local needs, forged through consensus, and built upon each school's unique strengths. A combination of strategies is necessary to achieve a new vision of learning. The goal is not to make each school the same; it is to enable each school to construct its own solutions. The solutions must be consistent with rigorous and relevant education and supported by positive relationships with students.

Change must begin with community expectations. Improvement efforts at the school must reflect the community's needs. Leaders need a plan and a set of tools for working with people throughout the process of change. Facilitating change requires having the right strategies and techniques working effectively – and at the right time – with people to create change. The International Center's work with leading schools across the country found a number of common characteristics in the successful process of change:

- Change must be revolutionary in spirit, yet evolutionary in time frame. Gradual change has a higher rate of acceptance and success than "quick fix" change.
- Each school community is unique; what works in one does not necessarily work in another. Schools can survey the broad range of success stories from other systems and then choose or develop options that will work best in their specific situations.

- Schools tend to maintain the status quo. They often produce unintended consequences in response to change. Implementing change for change's sake is a hit-or-miss proposition. A more successful approach is to first define the problems or issues a school faces, then tailor responses to address those specific circumstances.
- As with any system, schools produce the results they are designed to produce. If different results are desired, the focus must be on changing the system, not simply demanding that the system work better.
- School change can occur when it is guided by leadership, driven by data, and supported through continuous professional learning.

Administrators and staff in the most successful schools embrace change as exciting and challenging, rather than as intimidating and threatening. These educators understand that schools today must be updated in order to keep pace with a changing society and economy.

Why Change Schools?

The driving force to improve U.S. schools must come from a recognition that our schools are not adequately preparing students for their futures. The skills individuals will need to succeed in this century are much different from those required in the past. American society is undergoing fundamental, structural changes at the family, workplace, and community levels, and our education system must evolve as well.

Parents and community leaders must also understand that, in many cases, the skills, knowledge, and behaviors needed for entry-level employment today outstrip those needed to enter higher education. Our nation's persistent fixation on preparing young people for college – while a worthy goal – can become an impediment to achieving world-class education standards. Certainly we must continue to prepare our young people to be good citizens and ready them for higher education. However, parents and others must recognize that we must add a third important purpose to education: learning to apply academic skills needed for the increasingly sophisticated workplace. Next, parents and community leaders must be convinced that schools need to change. Then we will be able to create the type of pressure needed to support moving the curriculum to a more relevant skill base.

School districts that have been successful in creating an environment that supports change have used a variety of techniques. Those include print media, radio, and television; special events and presentations; community partnerships; and student and parent focus forums. As discussed in Chapter 1, successful schools work to address the four mega-trends of globalization, demographics, technology, and changing attitudes and values.

While Americans as a group seem convinced that this country's schools must change, most parents and taxpayers believe schools are just fine as they are. Higher-performing schools understand clearly the realities of our changing society. Rather than feeling threatened by those changes, these schools understand the *why* and embrace the need for schools to evolve. They take the necessary steps to help their communities understand these new realities.

What Needs to Change in Schools?

The goal of providing a challenging curriculum requires us to rethink the traditional assumptions of how schools operate. Schools and communities across the nation are taking bold initiatives to redesign learning. What common elements do those successful efforts share? Based on its research, during the 2003-2004 school year, the International Center identified 10 key components for improving schools. These have since been refined to include the eight components outlined in Chapter 1, but the original components were:

1. Culture of High Expectations and Support – Create a culture that embraces the belief that *all* students can benefit from a rigorous and relevant curriculum and

provides personalized relationships between adults and students to support high levels of achievement

2. Data-driven Decisions – Use data to provide a clear, unwavering focus to curriculum priorities that are both rigorous and relevant, instruction that is personalized, and school improvement that is continuous

3. Accountability – Set high expectations that are monitored, and then hold both students and adults accountable for students' continuous improvement in the curriculum priorities

4. Articulated Curriculum – Use a framework to organize curriculum that drives instruction toward both rigor and relevance and leads to a continuum of instruction between grades and across disciplines

5. Rigorous and Relevant Instruction – Teach students through experiences that are challenging; stimulate reflective thought, and are real-world applications of skills and knowledge

6. Personalized Learning – Create appropriate transitions into and from school and multiple pathways to rigor and relevance based upon a student's interests, learning style, aptitude, and needs

7. Professional Learning Communities – Foster development of a highly collaborative staff and provide sustained professional development focused on the improvement of instruction

8. Partnerships – Obtain and leverage parent and community involvement resulting in positive relationships with schools

9. School Climate – Establish and maintain a safe and orderly school

10. Leadership – Offer effective leadership development for administrators, teachers, parents, and community

In 2004, the International Center – in conjunction with the Council of Chief State School Officers and with the financial support of the Bill & Melinda Gates Foundation – conducted a study about the most successful high schools in the country.

The study sought to understand the characteristics that made these schools effective. Our investigation identified nine central characteristics of high performing schools:

1. instruction focused around students' interests, learning styles and aptitudes through a variety of small learning community approaches, most commonly through academies
2. an unrelenting commitment by administrators and teachers to excellence for all students, with a particular emphasis on literacy across the curriculum
3. a laser-like focus on data at the classroom level to make daily instructional decisions for individual students
4. an extraordinary commitment of resources and attention to 9th grade students
5. a rigorous and relevant 12th grade year
6. high-quality curriculum and instruction that focuses on rigor, relevance, relationships, and reflective thought
7. solid and dedicated leadership
8. relationships driven by guiding principles
9. sustained and supported professional development

This research clearly illustrates that schools need to build rigor, relevance, and relationships. This is more than a new alliteration for the 3Rs of learning. The new 3Rs are embedded in almost all of the characteristics on this list, a summary of the *what* of school reform.

How Do We Change Schools?

Once schools go through the process of discovering *why* they must change, they next analyze data that identifies *what* they must change. This reflection will better position them for deciding *how* they need to change. Dealing with *how* to change, however, remains the most difficult part of the reform process. Schools that communicate the *why* to everyone and build agreement around the *what* are well on their way to success. However, implementing the *how* is a challenge that frustrates many school leaders.

The real challenge is breaking free of traditions and assumptions that have become standard operating procedures in our schools. Successful schools create an environment where educators and students at every level feel safe in questioning current practices and procedures. To maintain success over a long period of time, schools need to engage constantly in reflective thinking. They must question and evaluate not only their established ideas, strategies, procedures, and programs, but also their more recent improvements. Truly successful schools possess a restlessness and ongoing passion for continuous improvement. They shy away from complacency, seeking instead to continually strive to improve and reinvent themselves. They realize that school reform is an ongoing process, not an event.

Leaders of change in high-performing schools are willing to take risks because they believe change is the best choice. They know that improving education requires both individuals to change and for organizational changes to be made. They understand that playing it safe – standing still – is more dangerous than taking a risk.

Change does not come easily or swiftly. Simply attempting to adopt and implement a best practice from a model school does not work. Figuring out how to help people adapt to change and implement best practices requires skillful intervention by school leaders who are agents of change.

Money, time, regulations, and other factors are often viewed as barriers to change. However, they are not true barriers; they are symptoms of people's attitudes. The only real obstacles are people who resist change. Leaders who seek to become agents of change must sharpen their people skills because facilitating change is all about working effectively with people.

Successful schools have demonstrated that the best way to develop innovative practices is to involve as many people as possible in formulating new education plans. This means not only staff and administration, but also parents, students, and other community members. Consensus building through these constituents is not a quick and efficient process, but it does yield a better, longer lasting result. Shared decision making generates a larger pool of ideas. Once consensus is reached, the process builds ownership and commitment to ensure those plans are carried out and supported.

Transformation succeeds if people affected by the change feel ownership of the change. People often welcome change; change can be powerful, exciting, and positive. But people resist changes when they feel they have no say in or control over it. Ideally, the goal is not to figure out how to convince people to accept change, but rather to figure out how to scaffold the change process in such a way that people can be part of the process and feel that they can have some influence on the outcomes.

In starting the process, it can be helpful to consider the nature of schools as a unique system. Some consider schools to be organized around an industrial model of mass-production, an assembly line with a constantly moving conveyor belt that aims to produce student "products" that meet specific quality measurements. Schools that attempt to convey the same knowledge to each student in the same way over the same period of time use a process similar to that for manufacturing an appliance.

However, our studies show that schools that use this outdated industrial model are not the most successful ones. Certainly, we must maintain some universal minimum requirement for learning basic skills, but we must also be able to personalize learning so students can learn at different speeds and experiences. Learning is now seen as a more organic, natural, and unpredictable process than it used to be. Current brain research indicates that a child's learning is more like a growing plant that gradually absorbs nutrients, adds stems and leaves, and seeks equilibrium in the world. School can be considered a sort of biological process in which we create an environment for good learning and good teaching so we can effectively nurture students.

Similarly, the traditional approach to school improvement also has been based on an "optimal manufacturing process" tactic. Phrases such as "building capacity," "measuring success," and "replicating models" indicates a belief that we can reform schools by putting together various building blocks more efficiently. Perhaps our lack of success in implementing school change more broadly is that our approach prevents us from recognizing the true characteristics of schools and the ways in which we can act to stimulate change within them.

While schools traditionally may be designed around a mass production model, we know that the nuances that individuals – teachers and students – bring to the process of education are essential. Changing the culture within a school is much more dynamic and complicated than merely constructing a new building. To improve schools, we need to discard the old physical planning model and think differently by using a biological model. A fitting phrase to describe such a biological framework is "learning from life." We know that biological organisms are influenced heavily by the community around them, and results cannot be predicted or planned. This is similar to schools, which are complex and constantly changing as staff and students come and go, or as expectations change.

A Case Study of the *How*

In the late 1990s, the Wake County Public School System (WCPSS) in North Carolina formulated a "stretch goal." This ambitious plan forced educators and the community at large to think beyond what was achievable with already-available resources. The school district created this stretch goal using input from the business sector, parent groups, teacher organizations, and its division of principals and assistant principals, among numerous other groups.

WCPSS wanted to identify a goal that would satisfy these myriad stakeholders. What single, overarching goal would these diverse groups all recognize as one that would reflect the purpose of public education, be meaningful to all citizens, and set a lofty standard for achievement? The process of collecting this input inspired the community to support the school system.

In the summer of 1998, WCPSS established Goal 2003. The goal stated: "By 2003, 95 percent of students tested in grades 3 and 8 will be at or above grade level as measured by the North Carolina End-of-Grade tests."

Did you notice that this goal stated that 95 percent of *all* students – African-American, Asian, Caucasian, Latino/Hispanic, Native American, academically gifted, academically struggling,

69

those receiving free/reduced lunch benefits, etc. – would be above grade level? Although the goal was set to measure success of students in grades 3 and 8, all grade levels would be affected over the course of the five years set for achieving the goal. Third grade teachers would want the K-2 teachers to prepare students for the 3rd grade, and the 8th grade teachers would want the same of the earlier grade level teachers, too. High school teachers surely would want the district to achieve success, and wouldn't it be nice to work with students who were better prepared for the secondary grades?

It is important to note that WCPSS had settled on a single goal. Whereas many school districts create a lengthy collection of goals, trying to address a great variety of desired outcomes, this district identified one, easy-to-remember goal that represented the sum of everything it hoped to accomplish with students. What's more, no additional funding was associated with this goal.

To many people in the community, the 95 percent goal seemed absurd. For some population groups and regions of the county, with percentages in the 60s and 70s, this goal seemed unrealistic. Such a goal was surely unachievable, they thought, so why set up the district for failure and community ridicule? Even if the goal was attainable, how could such progress be made by 2003, in only five years? Why not set a more realistic goal? How about 85 percent or even 90 percent? Still, there were many other individuals who believed that the notion of raising achievement for all students in the entire district was an exciting challenge.

Reaching Goal 2003 called for a strategic plan unlike any that had been designed and implemented in the school system before. Dramatic work needed to be done if all students were to make this mark. The majority students – Caucasian – were performing about 10 percentage points below the 95 percent level, and the minority students – in particular, African-American and Latino/ Hispanic students – were performing well below that. Factor in other population groups, such as students with disabilities, free- or reduced-lunch recipients, and English language learners, and one can easily see that this was indeed a daunting task. But was this new goal daunting and foolish, or was it a daunting yet courageous undertaking? School leaders did not know the answer, but they were committed to the standard of accountability, and they moved forward to make it happen.

The goal energized all facets of the community with its single focus. Each group could see its worth and the impact it would have on their children. African-American and Latino/Hispanic families could see a commitment to improve the academic standing of their children; at the same time, Caucasian and Asian families could be sure their children's needs would be addressed as well. The challenge was trying to close the achievement gap while ensuring that advanced students could grow academically as well. Resources could not be taken from the best performing students to help the lower performing students. Any perception that the best and brightest students would not be served was aggressively countered, knowing that such a perception could result in the defection of these students to private, parochial, charter, or home schools. In adopting the goal, the district could end up damaging itself if it led parents to withdraw their children from the district.

One measure of the success achieved in pursuit of Goal 2003 was in securing new resources and making better use of existing ones. While Goal 2003 was set with the knowledge that additional resources were not guaranteed, over time, the goal became a mantra for organizing the resources needed to achieve the mission. Subsequently, the Wake County Board of County Commissioners appropriated additional funds; school administrators reviewed all budget items to identify funds to support the goal. Through the effort of the commissioners and realignment of existing school district resources, the district was able to cover a portion of the new and expanded strategies that it was beginning to roll out in pursuit of the goal, without major tax increases.

The success of Goal 2003 was evident in the achievement gains the district's students made. From 1994 to 2003, the composite percentage of 3rd and 8th grade students who passed both of North Carolina's reading and mathematics end-of-grade exams rose from 75.7 percent to 91.3 percent. While the district did not completely achieve the 95 percent goal, its progress was nothing less than remarkable. Each of the district's major racial

71

population groups made steady gains over those years. The achievement gap – about 40 percentage points – that existed in 1994 between the highest and lowest performing groups narrowed to fewer than 20 percentage points by 2003. It is especially impressive that all population groups made steady gains, from the highest performing population groups to the lowest performing ones.

Goal 2003 shows what can happen when school leaders, schools, and communities choose to put themselves to the test and elevate expectations for all students. The approach has plenty of critics. The process was not easy for teachers, administrators, students, or parents. There was hard work, dedication, and need to be constantly on guard for the negativism that so often pervades the school culture. But, in the end, the results speak for themselves.

Strategies for Changing Schools

At the International Center, we have developed a model to implement school change. The model is divided into six phases, each with unique change strategies. These strategies represent the approaches or group techniques that should be used at the appropriate times.

Envision: Dream the Possible

By envisioning, people come to believe things can be different. Through the vision of a strong leader, people can imagine what it would be like to have problems solved, for processes to run more smoothly, or for outcomes to be more successful. When change is imposed, it is often opposed. Envisioning reduces the tendency for opposition.

Discover: Focus on the Organization's Competence

Discovery involves posing tough questions to help people think about the positive aspects of the organization related to the vision. Instead of starting with negative talk about what is wrong with the school, you begin by looking closely at the school's strengths. Reflecting on success stories and posing "what if" scenarios can help staff discover what is possible through organizational change.

Create: Design Solutions Through Kaleidoscope Thinking

Creating solutions requires getting people to think in innovative ways by considering as many different ideas and perspectives as possible. The purpose of this strategy is to expand people's perspectives and generate novel and unique solutions to problems. Divergent thinking is healthy; it should be deliberately planned and embraced.

Build: Forge a Consensus for Change

This reference to "building" is the opposite of creating. Its purpose is to get people thinking alike by building consensus. In this strategy, it is important to develop plans and activities to achieve a common vision. Enough details must be in place to determine the resources necessary to start implementation. However, it is good for some details to be left out. This provides the opportunity to engage more people in defining the specifics.

Develop: Cultivate the Growth of People

Change will not succeed unless people develop the skills necessary to understand change. This strategy also refers to building good communication. People will participate more actively and learn more if they understand the nature of the change. Developing is not about formal professional development workshops, although they may be useful. Rather, developing is about setting a climate in which staff has rich opportunities to learn and share experiences. People must feel free to take risks and try new things. In this type of environment, staff will grow and develop.

Support: Sustain People through Implementation

Support is the most neglected strategy, and this neglect often limits the impact of a change. People are naturally tentative when making a change. To be sure that implementation continues, people in the organization who are struggling to adopt the change will need follow-up and coaching. For those who are successful, rewards and recognition are valuable in reinforcing the change and making people feel good about it. Financial resources must not be forgotten when providing assistance for change. Too many good ideas have been labeled "ineffective" because there was not adequate ongoing support for implementing the change.

Each of these six strategies is critical to organizational change. They apply to many aspects of education, from changes in teaching to learning to building a new school building. The phases fall into a logical order. However, things rarely go smoothly in the real world and organizations often must revisit a phase to correct a weakness. If any of the phases is not carried out effectively, problems will arise. Leaders must be able to sense where people are in the organization and what their needs are. Leaders must focus on the correct strategy for working with people and select the right tools.

All these strategies aim to answer some basic question of where to start. Where are we now? Where are we heading? These questions demand answers in concrete, quantifiable terms to support the ultimate goal of changing our schools.

In this change model, the answers to these questions are driven by knowing where you want to end up as a result. Begin with the end in mind. Without a destination, one road is as good as another. Schools need to know where they are going before they try to get there. While this may seem like common sense, most schools do not begin with a clear picture of what their desired student results are. Instead, schools jump into changes and solutions because changing something, adopting a practice that has worked elsewhere, for instance, seems like the right thing to do. It seems proactive and responsive. While schools do need change, changing too quickly or attempting to make changes without a clear destination will not be effective.

Even in the best of schools, there is still a need to change, and good leaders sense this. This sense may result from knowledge that the school failed to serve some students adequately or because of unsatisfactory results on a state assessment. Change, to most school leaders, seems to be about making things incrementally better. Most believe there are many good things going on instructionally in their school, so they try to change a few things to address the visible problem, say, the fact that a few students are not succeeding. Other leaders think small changes are easier for the staff to accept. Being too cautious, however, can lead to staff dissatisfaction if it appears that things are not really changing or that they are not changing for the better. Practices such as eliminating recess and reducing instruction in the arts to allow for more instructional time before assessments have occurred in schools – to the detriment of students. Schools need to be cautious in making changes when the measures of success are so very narrow.

The problem is that many schools have simply accepted federal and state mandates as their accountability measures. Schools must be more proactive. Governments only set a few measures of school success, so schools should design their own, more comprehensive set of measures to determine their effectiveness, a process discussed in greater detail in Chapter 7.

This is the *where* of change: examining where a school is heading. Attempting change with only a few narrow measures, such as test scores, will not result in great schools. Ultimately, this approach will force schools to discontinue practices that are important and valuable parts of learning. Schools must change with the awareness of where the school is heading – where they want it to be heading – and know how it will measure success. The clarity and comprehensive nature of school accountability measures should drive changes around locally developed goals that enable continuous measurement of success.

This is where the Learning Criteria to Support 21st Century Learners, discussed in Chapter 2, comes in. The Learning Criteria provides an opportunity for schools to translate their beliefs about teaching and learning into measurable goals. Educators can and must step back and redefine learning measures in a more comprehensive manner, one that is not limited to state test results. This will enable educators to embrace goal setting and accountability measures that are more consistent with what they believe about teaching and learning.

Educators can focus on the need for revised accountability measures by considering such questions as:

- How do you identify school success?
- How do you describe an "educated student" in your school?
- Are state tests the only thing that matters? If not, what else matters?
- Does being judged strictly on state test results narrow your work focus?
- How do you really measure whether school improvements are working?
- How can you focus your community on the needs of students?
- Do current measures of student learning fail to identify some of your best students?

The Learning Criteria's four categories – core academic learning, stretch learning, learner engagement, and personal skill development – guide the data collection and analysis process to help school leaders determine the success of their schools in preparing students for current assessments as well as future roles and responsibilities. These steps support the approach that the place to begin change is not with best practices, but with a clear vision of the desired end results. By having comprehensive indicators of student learning, a school is better prepared to select, adapt, and implement best practices that truly will make a difference in student learning.

Bringing the Pieces Together:
Principles and Strategy Considerations

To recap, the model for school change is built around three major facets:
- aspiring for rigor, relevance, and relationships
- beginning with the end in mind
- thinking about schools as biological systems

These facets form the core of the change model. In addition, there are 13 principals of change that schools can focus on when implementing desired changes:

- make decisions based on data, not opinions
- enlist passionate people who see the possibilities
- focus on fluency in literacy
- grow staff through professional learning opportunities
- hold teams accountable for learning results
- inspire innovative instruction; instruction matters more than structure
- join with the community to form true partnerships
- know your students and know your strengths
- develop and live by lofty expectations
- measure learning by proficiency
- nurture positive relationships
- offer multiple pathways to achievement
- prioritize the curriculum; remember, less is more

These principles form the basis for the actions leaders need to take to implement change through people. There are many techniques for working with individuals and groups outlined for each of the six phases in the previous section. A good leader will adjust his or her style and activities depending on the strategy being used. The six strategies for changing schools, along with tips for leaders to use to keep the process focused and to help each phase move smoothly toward success, are:

1. Envision: Dream the Possible
   - focus on the future
   - do not lay blame
   - paint mental pictures
   - use metaphors
   - be enthusiastic
   - keep the message simple
   - repeat, repeat, repeat

2. Discover: Focus on the Organization's Competence
   - focus on the positive
   - reflect on what works well
   - develop mental images of high performance
   - ask "what if" questions

- tell success stories about personal development
- focus on and work from what is known

3. Create: Design Solutions through Kaleidoscope Thinking
   - encourage divergent thinking
   - build trust
   - provide extensive information
   - use brainstorming
   - allow open participation
   - recognize that it is okay to feel uncomfortable

4. Build: Forge a Consensus for Change
   - encourage convergent thinking
   - give adequate lead time
   - use consensus decision making
   - provide situational leadership
   - be empathetic to human needs

5. Develop: Cultivate the Growth of People
   - use outside people to start
   - use inside people to carry out
   - provide "just in time" development
   - encourage and support personal development
   - use skilled communicators
   - keep communication simple
   - get verbal commitment to change from all parties involved

6. Support: Sustain People through Implementation
   - provide adequate resources
   - give recognition and rewards
   - evaluate and revise
   - consider individual differences
   - provide follow-up
   - expect results and inspect progress

Overall, remember that one way to be an effective leader and agent of change is to take the right action at the right time. Naturally, the right action depends on the symptoms of your organization and where the school is in the change process. The symptoms often reflect which phase of the process requires your focus:

- If people are apathetic and uncommitted, focus on the envision phase.
- If people are unproductive and have low morale, focus on discovery.
- If people have tunnel vision or remain committed to the status quo, focus on creation.
- If people are confused, anxious, or conflicted, focus on the build phase.
- If people are fearful, frustrated, and lack confidence, focus on development.
- If people are tentative, are discouraged, or are slow implementers, focus on support.

Again, organizations are made up of people. Becoming a leader and a successful facilitator of school change is about working effectively with people. By clearly understanding this and developing the skills to work with groups and individuals, leaders can become agents of change and help to create the schools our children deserve.

CHAPTER FOUR

A Balancing Act:

Clarifying Student Learning Expectations

How do schools decide what to take off the plate in their overcrowded curriculum? How do schools determine an appropriate level of proficiency to expect all students to achieve in the skills and knowledges that are taught?

These seem like very black and white questions, ones that we should easily be able to answer. As schools and state departments of education tackle these two critical questions, however, we find there is actually a great deal of uncertainty and emotional debate surrounding these queries.

Successful schools find a way around conflicts. They typically begin by determining what will be included on their state's test. With that information, they are able to clearly define which standards or subset of standards – often called benchmarks, student expectations, or objectives – to focus curriculum and instruction on.

While it may be difficult to obtain it, information for each state testing program in the country is usually available. Throughout the country, schools need this information; schools that are persistent enough obtain it. At the International Center, we have worked hard to answer the test question for each state so that, through the Curriculum Matrix, we may share pertinent information with the schools we work with. With today's politically driven, media intensive spotlight focused on student performance on state tests, schools must assure that students do well on the test before they do anything else. The problem with focusing on this question is that it leads schools to simply prepare students for the test.

Schools must define their expectations for student learning so that they may define what will be taught. Once a determination is made as to which student expectations should be taught, the critical question arises: what level of proficiency indicates success? A June 2007 National Assessment of Educational Progress (NAEP) study, *Mapping 2005 State Proficiency Standards onto the NAEP Scales*, shows that there is enormous variation among states' definitions of proficiency. It is clear that simply crossing a state line does not dramatically change the level of reading, writing, or math proficiency an individual needs for success in higher education, the workplace, the home, or in life. Therefore, the International Center conducted two national studies – the Lexile Framework® for Reading literacy study and the Quantile Framework® for Mathematics study – to define the needed level of proficiency for success beyond the classroom.

The results clearly pointed out that, in most school districts in every state, expectations are far too low in the area of literacy. The reading requirements in the workplace and the home are dramatically higher than they are in our schools and colleges. In mathematics, the study showed that math requirements needed for adult roles are not as great as those required in high schools, the opposite conclusion of the reading study. Therefore, the biggest challenge is identifying those math skills that essential and the working to ensure that students master those. But how do schools go about fixing these literacy and mathematics gaps?

Narrowing the Field: Using the Curriculum Matrix

In the past, gathering educational data was a slow, unwieldy, and impractical process. Today's technology makes the widespread use of data for decision making both possible and practical at every level of the system. Students, teachers, parents, administrators, and community partners have access to meaningful information about performance. Educators are embracing performance data as a useful means to focus and direct achievement.

Many schools that struggle to improve proficiency for all students are data-rich but analysis-poor. However, the most successful schools focus on their instructional data to answer two questions:

- What is on the test?
- What will students need to know and be able to do once they leave school?

Answering these questions is critical for setting instructional and curricular priorities. True, data-driven achievement involves more than reacting to low test scores. Schools and teachers must acquire and analyze more than the results of standardized tests in order to improve student performance.

Many educators are more comfortable basing decisions on subjective judgments rather than on statistics. Subjective decisions are often appropriate because there are so many variables that influence teaching. At the same time, however, educators can best improve the quality of instruction by focusing on concrete, objective data. Data-driven instruction uses quantifiable data to determine what is important to teach. This data – both state testing results and other types of information – does not define or even limit the entire scope of teaching; rather, data gives focus to what's happening in a classroom.

Successful schools equip students with the skills and knowledge necessary not simply to achieve academic success, but also to become lifelong learners and successful adults. Student test scores are only one measure of progress toward those goals. In order to plan instruction that gives students the best possible education, teachers must know what the standards are, which are tested, and which are considered essential.

To assess how well students are doing, educators must look at a variety of sources that provide evidence of student performance. Classroom-based measures include profiles, portfolios, exhibitions, projects, diagnostic assessments, and assessments that cover subject skills, concepts, and knowledge. Another source is norm-referenced – or criterion-referenced – standardized tests, which supplement state tests. Evidence can also be gathered by reviewing classroom performance, report cards, student records, and other performance indicators. Teachers need to identify which data to collect and decide how to analyze that data to support the ultimate goal of focusing school improvement efforts.

Data supports the basic question so many teachers face today: What should we teach? Teachers and administrators are often overwhelmed by the numerous – and sometimes conflicting – standards for which they are held responsible. Most curricula contain more content than can be reasonably taught during a school year. Nonetheless, educators feel intense pressure to have their students meet state testing requirements while also preparing pupils for participation in life after graduation.

There is no simple answer to the question of what to teach in an overcrowded curriculum. But districts can begin by articulating a clear vision for a quality education. That vision should be based on what students must know and be able to do. Content is critical when students will need that knowledge for future success or when they will be tested on the knowledge and skills. Sometimes, these needs co-exist. All stakeholders in the district must share in the vision of a quality education as it will guide all performance improvement efforts throughout the system.

To assist educators in determining what should be taught, The International Center developed the Curriculum Matrix, which combines results from the National Essential Skills Study, or NESS (see Chapter 2), with state standards and learning expectations for English language, arts, mathematics, and sciences. The matrix contains the core data that a district or an individual school needs in order to determine what to teach and how to raise test scores.

The Curriculum Matrix is based on a state's standards. Most states divide their standards into general statements of learning expectations and subcategories. The subcategories may be called key ideas, performance indicators, benchmarks, topics, learning outcomes, or grade-level expectations. The general category is stated as a broad goal or outcome statement or as an identified content area.

The subcategories have the greatest impact on instructional decision making since they give more detail regarding what a student must know or be able to do to meet the standard. Often topics suggest appropriate instructional activities. Educators must be familiar with the categories and topics in their state standards so they can help students and parents understand how and why instructional decisions have been made.

The second component of the Curriculum Matrix is selected state assessments. All tests required by the *No Child Left Behind Act of 2001* (NCLB) for grades 3 through 8 are included in the matrix. This tool also includes at least one high school level test in English language arts, math, and science. The topics in the relevant standards are then correlated to the testing specifications or related test items. Topics are rated as high, medium, or low based on the extent to which those topics are tested. This provides a general guideline that schools can use to determine which topics are priorities in their state testing program.

A third component of the matrix is the significance of topics in the standards as they relate to the NESS. The NESS reflects expectations of educators, members of the business community, parents, and the general public about the skills and knowledge students should have when they graduate from high school. State standards topics are also assigned ratings of high, medium, or low based on the cross-reference to the NESS and how an essential skill ranks.

The final step in the Curriculum Matrix is assigning an overall priority rating to each topic. This rating is determined from the topic's correlation to the state test and to the essential skills. An item is rated low if it is not included on the test, and/ or if it is correlated to a low-priority essential skill. In a similar fashion, items that link to state tests and essential skills get the highest ratings, with items relating to only one of those areas tending to fall in the middle. Educators can use these priority ratings to make informed decisions about whether to place more or less emphasis on individual topics.

Once the analysis is completed, educators can move into setting instructional priorities. Teachers first need to understand their state standards, know which topics are essential, and determine which topics are on the test. That information helps them set the next steps to help move toward rigor, relevance, and student success.

Translating those standards into student learning experiences involves a critical shift from the question, "What shall I teach?" to "What must the students learn?" Teachers within the same grade level or high school department can begin by identifying skills and knowledge that students need to learn within that grade or discipline. Of course, even with all the appropriate tools and information, instructional planning is a complex process that goes beyond simply selecting a textbook chapter and making it an instructional topic. There are many factors to consider, including:

- standards
- teacher content knowledge
- community expectations
- student knowledge
- teacher self-knowledge
- assessment practices
- instructional strategies

Each of these factors involves the classroom teacher using his or her professional judgment. Lesson plans can be built by others that relate directly to standards. Teachers at the district level can develop curriculum maps and ideas. The other factors, however, are best added at the school level by the teacher who can make these fine adjustments to ensure that the lesson plan is appropriate to his or her own group of students. Steps in the instructional planning process include:

- making instructional unit/curriculum connections that tie the plan to curriculum standards and disciplines; items that will be tested or are measured as important to the public should receive priority

- setting expected levels of student knowledge and performance, as determined by both standardized testing and other school criteria
- identifying student work that meets expected skills and knowledge levels, as defined by the expected levels of student knowledge and performance described above
- creating a balance between content knowledge and its application in the outside world
- posing essential questions and concepts as a starting point to the instructional unit
- determining the assessment and instruction of expected skills and knowledge

Collecting these instructional plans becomes the operational curriculum. This is what the student will experience in the classroom as they work toward the mapped curriculum, which gives the standards that students will achieve. As teachers plan, they need to contemplate the many ways to reach the destination of student achievement and then select the most appropriate strategies depending upon the situation. Teachers who plan instruction effectively will have clear goals in mind for students. Although teachers tend to judge the quality of their work based on delivery of the lesson, quality instructional planning addresses the real measure of success: student learning.

Make It Count:
What You *Do* Teach, Teach to a Proficiency Level
That Kids Need

Teachers are challenged to examine basic assumptions in reading and mathematics as they move instruction and assessment to high levels of relevance, as defined by the Application Model and quadrants B and D of the Rigor/Relevance Framework (see Chapter 2). First, it is nearly impossible to avoid interdisciplinary instruction when designing relevant, real-world learning. Any real-world application of history or science naturally requires application of mathematics or language skills. At the outset, this appears to be a plus by creating opportunities to reinforce the basic application of reading and math. But proceed with caution, because the real world applies here.

Reading levels of textbooks and state reading tests are set by groups of teachers who are familiar with the current reading level of students in school. They subjectively set a level of comprehension that they feel students should rise to meet. Unfortunately, the process of setting such levels is often devoid of consideration of what is applicable to the real world. And that's the rub: the real world does not consider a student's level, it demands ability that is different from what is expected in a classroom.

We know that student learning styles are like fingerprints: they are different for everyone. Imagine a classroom situation where the teacher is lecturing or the students are reading a passage from a textbook. One can guess that only a fraction of the students are experiencing the appropriate amount of instructional material for the lesson to be effective. Students who find the lesson too rigorous become lost and discouraged. Other students may not be challenged enough and become bored.

Ideally, each student will experience measurable and sustained improvement from class to class, day to day, and grade to grade. By the time a student graduates from high school, he or she should have gained the requisite skills to succeed in the next stage of life, whether it is college or the workplace. If a student can step seamlessly into that next phase, then the education system has worked for that individual. If all students can make that transition, then the system on the whole is succeeding.

But we know this is not happening. In fact, it has not happened since long before the publication of *A Nation at Risk* in 1983, which, again, concluded that American schools were in danger of not preparing students to compete in the 21st century. NCLB is a continuation of the push for improved academic achievement and proficiency. But American education has responded by increasing academic rigor at the expense of developing a relevant skill set for this century. While there may be debate about the details, NCLB has traditionally had bipartisan political support and is likely to continue providing the framework for educational reform in this country.

In the early 1980s, the impetus for change came primarily from the business community, not from higher education, whose own slipping standards have allowed for more and more "developmental" English courses to backfill academic deficiencies among entering freshmen. Business and industry continue to feel firsthand the skills gap between what students are learning in school and what they actually need in order to be competitive in the modern, high-tech, global economy. The business community has long identified inadequate reading proficiency as a leading problem among entry-level employees. Educators have attempted to solve the problem by assigning more reading, mostly literature. The problem with this is twofold.

First, assigning more reading does not usually result in higher reading proficiency. A student at a certain reading level will not improve his proficiency unless he is continually challenged by the text. A student who reads a text that is at or below his reading level is not being challenged. Conversely, a student presented with a text well above her reading level will find it too complex and grow frustrated. A text needs to be slightly above a reader's ability level to promote growth in reading proficiency.

Second, prose is not read in most workplace situations. Literacy in the context of work requires better technical reading skills for understanding documents and quantitative material. Students need to be exposed to a variety of texts, not just from other content areas, but from career and technical education courses, personal-use or adult-roles texts, and sample occupational materials. The modern definition of literacy needs to encompass all types of text: prose, document, technological, and quantitative.

Now consider mathematics, which presents a slightly different scenario. Research is very preliminary as to the level of application of mathematics in most workplace settings. What is clear is that there are vast differences among career clusters, and there is less of an opportunity to generalize across careers about the real-world applications. One observation at the high school level is that mathematics instruction is out of step with interdisciplinary and real-world application. In most learning experiences in career and technical areas, economics, or science, the mathematics that are most often required are fractions, measurement, or statistics. When seeking opportunities to collaborate with a high school math teacher, a career and technical, economics, or science instructor may be told something along the lines of "That was covered in earlier grades, and we have moved on to . . ." Unfortunately, the earlier "coverage" by mathematics teachers has not prepared students with the application and fluency necessary to do the real-world math in these subjects. Teachers in related subjects often end up re-teaching math concepts to enable students to complete their work.

If we want our students to compete in the global marketplace, we must continue to strengthen the relationship between what the world is telling us it will require of students and what we are presenting in the classroom. Without this connection and continuity, students, whether entering college or the workforce, will be unprepared to meet the demands placed on them. Moreover, their lack of preparedness will have negative impacts on business and industry. Remember the effects of globalization we talked about in Chapter 1? Companies will continue to shift jobs overseas if they can pay workers in other countries less for the same – or higher – level of competence than young Americans can offer.

The Lexile Framework® for Reading

The challenge of reading is not simply with postsecondary education; the real world requires substantially higher levels of reading proficiency than most students possess. I touched briefly on the Lexile Framework for Reading in Chapter 2 in the discussion of essential skills and their role in the creation of relevant and rigorous curricula. The International Center, recognizing the essential need to create appropriate continuity between the classroom and the world beyond it, has used the framework as a tool to research the level of reading required in the real world.

Lexile measures, as components of the incremental Lexile scale, allow for measurement of both text difficulty and reader ability on the same scale. This enables readers to be appropriately matched with books that will be both engaging and challenging. Unlike grade equivalent measures of readability, the Lexile scale is based on uniform increments from 200L to 2000L. Using this scale, an increment of 100L is constant in terms of increase in semantic and syntactic complexity; a one-grade difference expressed in traditional grade equivalents, however, is not. For example, the difference in reading difficulty between 3.2 and 4.2 may be much greater than the "one-grade" difference between 9.2 and 10.2. Moreover, Lexile measures avoid the problem of labeling reading expectations for a particular grade level; referencing Lexile measures also reinforces the notion that reading abilities differ broadly within any grade.

Findings of a comprehensive research study using the Lexile Framework were reported at the 2003 Model Schools Conference. The findings showed a gap between students' reading levels and real-world reading requirements. The greatest gap among texts analyzed was between the reading requirements of workplace materials and literature assigned in schools. The International Center conducted a detailed study of the readability levels of a wide array of print materials encountered in the workplace. These occupational reading materials were linked to the 16 Career Clusters defined by the U.S. Department of Education at three job levels: entry, intermediate, and advanced. Our Lexile analysis revealed that a large number of entry-level jobs have higher reading requirements than those required for high school graduation. Subsequent studies continue support these conclusions.

Consider the following list of interquartile ranges of Lexile measures (25th percentile to 75th percentile) of the texts analyzed as part of the 2003 study:

Sample Group	Interquartile Range of Lexile Measures
High School Literature	730-960L
First-year College Literature	815-1050L
High School Textbooks	960-1140L
First-year College Textbooks	1095-1320L

Sample Group	Interquartile Range of Lexile Measures
Armed Forces Texts	1170-1225L
Personal-use/Adult-roles Texts	1160-1358L
Entry-level Employment Texts	1170-1380L

Looking at this list, it is easy to see the reading challenge. Even more so than postsecondary education, the real world requires substantially higher levels of reading proficiency than most students possess. States need to be sure that the reading proficiency levels they set under NCLB account for not just traditional academic measures of reading competence at the high school level, but also the skills that make individuals employable and successful in their post-graduation lives. This broader view of reading competency is an example of the academic proficiency that must become part of program improvement, so it is important to address this wherever possible in the curriculum.

The Quantile Framework® for Mathematics

Mathematics has its own framework – The Quantile Framework for Mathematics – to measure mathematical ability. The framework consists of a common supplemental unit of measure, the Quantile, to define mathematical ability. The Quantile measure for materials is a number indicating the mathematical demand of the material in terms of the concept/ application solvability. The Quantile measure for an individual or student is the level at which he or she is ready for instruction (50 percent competency with the material) and has knowledge of the prerequisite mathematical concepts and skills necessary to succeed. The Quantile scale ranges from Emerging Mathematician (0 Quantiles and below) to above 1400 Quantiles for the content typically taught in algebra II, geometry, and precalculus.

In addition to the Lexile study with high-performing schools, the International Center also asked the schools to submit a variety of math lessons used in their classrooms – in high school and the first year of college – as well as materials that involve mathematics found in their communities, including personal-use or adult-roles materials and employment materials from local businesses.

The initial findings are remarkable. The mathematical demand of high school and first-year college lesson materials far exceed the demands of employment and personal-use or adult-roles materials; this is a complete reversal of the skills gap in reading. Why? The math we use in our daily lives and even in our jobs simply does not typically involve the rigorous demands of a high school lesson. Naturally, some occupations require mastery of precalculus and algebra II; but on the whole, most do not. The math we do in our personal lives is even less rigorous.

These studies highlight the truly fundamental difference between reading and math. To become a lifelong learner and succeed in life, individuals must be reading literate in prose, document, and quantitative texts. Beyond high school, most individuals need only be math literate in day-to-day activities and in career-related mathematics, which varies widely by occupation. For instance, an accountant must have a great degree of statistics competency, while a good carpenter needs to be skilled in geometry.

The high rigor of high school mathematics courses is necessary to provide a well-rounded basis for students who may later decide to follow a particular career path based on his or her math aptitudes and interests. However, rigor needs to be balanced with relevance to make the instruction worthwhile for all students.

ABCs to DTQ:
Literacy for the 21st Century Global Workplace

How well are schools preparing students for the challenges of the new millennium? Remember what we said in Chapter 2? Valued employees in the 21st century must be creative problem-solvers and adaptive to change; they must interact fluidly with ever-changing technology, communicate, collaborate, and be highly literate. But are our students learning the skills they will need to complete their work, establish relationships, communicate, and collaborate in the work place? Many experts say education is failing at this critical task.

Workplace, community, and lifestyle reading is called "reading to act" or "reading to do." Schools provide students few opportunities to read, write, and communicate to act. Students spend no more than 25 percent of their time on literacy to act. Instead, instruction is focused on "learning literacy" – learning to read, write, speak, and listen – and "literacy to learn," which applies to content areas. But students leave schools for postsecondary education or to enter the workplace where 50 percent to 80 percent of all work-related tasks include document, technological, and quantitative (DTQ) forms of literacy. The result is that students enter postsecondary education or the workforce after high school and are expected to complete literacy tasks for which they are unprepared. While the literacy learning curve may decline as students gain experience, the initial learning curve will be very steep for most. Schools must do more to keep pace with rapid technology, research, and societal changes. They must embrace new designs for learning based on emerging research about how people learn, how to use technology effectively, and what skills are needed in the 21st century. We need to focus on skills and strategies that help all students access the future.

DTQ Literacy

In the United States, we are data rich and action poor. The data tells us consistently that we are underperforming with the DTQ forms of literacy that are essential to the global workplace. Among industrialized nations, The United States ranks poorly, even when comparing similar groups of high-achieving students or economically disadvantaged adults. Most of the 30 industrialized nations in the Organisation of Economic Co-operation and Development have a national effort geared toward DTQ literacy, but we do not. Continuing to follow this course will make it difficult to remain competitive globally. DTQ literacy is defined as:

- document literacy, which involves the skills needed to perform tasks associated with non-prose-based charts, maps, graphs, forms, tables, photos, video, Internet sources, and other visual materials; technological and quantitative forms of literacy support document literacy

- technological literacy, which refers to the ability to comprehend, use, solve, and create with Web-based information and sources, video-based information, or other multimedia information sources
- quantitative literacy, which involves the use of materials or sources that require mathematical understanding and the ability to solve problems or calculate answers.

Most teaching of DTQ literacy takes place in career and technical education programs. The strategies in this area are sometimes limited to literacy learning or content-area literacy. Such courses of study often involve students who are not considered to be on a track for college, but DTQ skills are not limited by economic, class, or educational boundaries. In the 21st century, *everyone* will need these skills to access security, economic well-being, communication, and health. We need a national mandate that we better prepare our students for the global stage.

Educators need to understand what level of skill their students are demonstrating in DTQ literacy. There are several ways to assess students' current performance in the areas of:

- assessing reading to do
- assessing writing to do
- assessing problem solving to do
- assessing and using technology to do

Once those assessments are completed, educators need to determine the DTQ literacy area (or areas) where students need the most assistance. This allows the teacher to select the most appropriate strategy to address the needs identified by the assessments.

But before they tackle DTQ literacy, educators first need to understand the similarities and differences in the kinds of literacy they currently teach. Content-area literacy is a particularly hot topic across the country, with some schools embracing the idea that learning content is a form of literacy. This is an incomplete approach, however. Students need more purpose-oriented and "active" literacy skills to be successful in the workplace and in postsecondary educational settings. The major aspects of DTQ literacy are:

- Previewing the document or source: Knowing what information is contained in a document, the source of the information, and how the information is presented allows the reader to locate or interact accurately with information in that document. Once the reader understands the construction of the document and the relationship to purpose, the task can be understood.

- Understanding the task: Readers interact with documents in order to do something with them. They need to know what they are being asked, what the purpose might be, and how the requested information or data match what they concluded the source contains. Matching format and content is an essential skill that requires high degrees of analysis. Once the task is understood, the reader can formulate a plan for the action to be completed.

- Completing the process: Readers now interact with the document to extract the needed information and complete their actions. Extracting information may be easy or complex, depending on the document and the task at hand. Quantitative-based sources also require some sort of problem solving to be performed. Once the process is completed, a reader can evaluate the results or success of the goal and the action plan.

These aspects point to the need for specific strategies to help teach the skills needed for DTQ forms of literacy. These strategies help students obtain the needed skills for workplace, lifestyle, and community literacy. Such approaches also work well in any content area that calls for mathematics; information in multiple forms; or the use of the Internet or other technologies.

Reading Proficiency for All

The importance of all students achieving reading proficiency – as well as federal requirements to set proficiency standards and monitor progress across subgroups of students – continues to influence policymakers, educators, and the American public. NCLB requires that all students be "proficient" in reading by the 2013-14 school year and demands that all schools make adequate yearly progress (AYP) toward that end. Proficiency is a truly worthy goal, but the practical realities of meeting it present some major challenges.

In the International Center's work with schools that have achieved substantial progress in the area of reading proficiency, we have learned some important lessons. First, while some schools have made great strides, success on a broad scale has remained elusive. Test scores and other criteria show that reading proficiency is simply not improving or is showing only modest change. Many schools and districts continue to struggle. Second, even where genuine successes have been realized, schools have recognized an important limitation: bringing all students to proficiency using the same strategies is highly unlikely no matter how many times the strategies are repeated. As Albert Einstein once remarked: "Insanity is doing the same thing over and over but expecting different results." Finally, some of the more successful districts have improved reading proficiency by developing and implementing K-12 literacy plans. Surprisingly few school districts have such plans. At best, they have a K-6 reading program. Most literacy plans begin with consideration of three questions:

1. What is reading proficiency?
2. How do we set reading proficiency standards?
3. What new approaches/techniques are needed to achieve reading proficiency for all?

What Is Reading Proficiency?

Lately, the International Center has been working extensively with several state departments of education and many individual school districts to answer the question: What is reading proficiency? Developing a clear definition of proficiency is not easy. Most schools use grade equivalents or passing scores on certain tests. Unfortunately, those numbers or scores relate only to academic benchmarks and norms that are unconnected to any observable external standards.

So we sought a common measurement tool to determine what students need to be able to read, what they *can* read, and what various assessment instruments measure. The Lexile Framework for Reading, discussed above, provides such a tool.

Lexile research points out what teachers already know, but it provides a consistent way to measure and address discrepancies. Students in the same classroom have different levels of reading proficiency, yet all of them are typically reading the same materials. Ask any teacher and they'll tell you that this results in a mismatch for many students. Students need textbooks they can read, especially in middle school and high school where there is a heavy reliance on textbooks as the primary instructional resource and source for learning.

For the past several decades, schools have placed a great deal of importance on pre-K-6 reading initiatives, a trend almost certain to continue accelerating because of NCLB. Little attention and few resources have been focused on students in grades 7 through 12, yet, these upper grades are exactly where emphasis is needed, according to recent international studies. The studies show that reading achievement of American 4th graders ranks among the best in the world. By 8th grade, American students' performance declines to around the international average. By 12th grade, our students rank even lower.

The basic question to ask is: "Why?" Reading demands increase dramatically for students around 4th grade, when learning begins to rely more on textbooks. The vocabulary encountered is less familiar because it contains more specialized or technical terms. Syntax becomes more complex. Inferential thinking and prior knowledge become the emphasis, and more independent learning is expected than in lower grades. This may seem counter to the statistics I just mentioned, which show American 4th graders ranking highly internationally in reading.

When reading becomes the primary vehicle for learning, the demands on readers and the strategies they need to use in reading change. Unfortunately, just when the reading load increases and students shift from learning to read to reading to learn, the scaffold of systematic and focused reading instruction diminishes or disappears altogether. No corresponding instruction in reading is provided to students. Student performances in reading begin to widen, and increasingly, schools begin to use more single-source instructional materials, such as textbooks and teacher handouts, for all students.

Thus, a gap emerges between the overall reading ability levels of students and the readability levels of the materials they are expected to read and understand. We must match students to instructional materials for more learning to occur.

Reading Instruction: Standards Versus the Real World

While a gap exists in secondary school between some students' reading levels and the instructional materials used, an even more alarming disconnect can be found between expected student levels and real-world reading requirements. The greatest gap occurs between students' present reading levels and the reading requirements of the workplace. Entry-level jobs today often have higher reading requirements than many of the more advanced positions in the same field. Moreover, while white-collar workers may spend more time reading on the job, the material that many blue-collar workers must read is often more complex and critically important to job performance; poor comprehension of technical manuals and installation instructions, for example, can have disastrous results.

By comparison with the entry-level occupational reading requirements, consider again the reading ability levels of our mid-range students in grades 10 through 12, as shown in the interquartile table for the Lexile Framework for Reading, above. There is a clear and alarming disparity between high school students' reading skills and the reading proficiency levels they need for work and for much of the reading they will do in their personal lives.

From Defining the Problem to Solving It

Our studies show that the real world requires substantially higher levels of reading proficiency than most students possess. States need to be sure that the reading proficiency levels they set under NCLB reflect not just traditional academic measures of reading competence, but also the larger picture of what individuals will need for employability and success in life after graduation. This broader view of reading competency is an example of the academic proficiency that must become part of program improvement under the law.

Can schools close the gap? The answer is: "Yes." The International Center has had the opportunity to work with selected schools that have experienced substantial success in closing the gap, and we have learned much from them. Among the lessons:

- Schools need to share with educators, parents, and the general public easy-to-understand data that explains the gap between where students are and where they need to be.
- The amount and complexity of reading that students must do increase dramatically at the secondary level. Educators need to initiate pre-K-12 literacy plans for all students with a strong emphasis on reading in the content areas in grades 7 through 12.
- Schools need to match students to instructional materials at appropriate reading levels.
- Schools need to provide comprehensive, well-focused, and sustained staff development that stresses the need for reading instruction that involves all teachers, with particular emphasis on teachers for grades 7 through 12 and the inherent benefits to their students' performance in the content area.
- Schools need an ongoing reading assessment system to measure students' continuous progress in reading, particularly as it relates to achieving AYP under NCLB.
- Schools need a way to compare where students are in reading and where they need to be to fulfill their educational and real-world goals and obligations. The Lexile Framework for Reading is an excellent tool to do this.

In the end, our information-based society demands high reading proficiency levels. We have data that defines what those demands are, and successful practices have been created to address them. Schools must use the resources available and address this critical area. We believe that K-12 literacy may be the best investment of energy and resources that schools can make. The human and economic consequences of not closing the gap – for our students and our country – are too severe to ignore.

CHAPTER FIVE

Methods, Not Madness:

Adopt Effective Instructional Practices

First Among Equals? The Primacy of Instruction

Let us begin with some historical context for this chapter. In 2007, we started thinking about creating the Components of School Excellence, a school improvement "framework" that we also use as the organizing principle for this book.

Working with my colleagues at the International Center for Leadership in Education, including Tim Ott, Ray McNulty, and Dick Jones — who are some of the best educators I know — and with advice and assistance from many other educators, I introduced the "list" in 2008. In forcing ourselves to even attempt to boil down the challenge of school improvement into a manageable "concept map," we drew upon the abundance of available research. However, in particular, we relied upon our collective decades (more than I would like to count) of experience and understandings gained from working with thousands of states, districts, and schools in recognizing the factors that have the greatest impact on sustainable school improvement.

As our thinking evolved, we debated whether the key ideas in the Components were "steps," "elements," or "events." We argued whether or not the Components represent a natural pattern or sequence that needed to be approached in order. We struggled over whether each Component was self-contained or overlapped other Components and to what extent. We asked ourselves if the process was linear, circular/cyclical, or should be pictured and shared with educators as some other visual representation and notion. Should the Components be numbered or just bulleted, lest they be misunderstood as a step-by-step panacea or formulaic how-to "assembly (or repair) manual" that, followed by rote, would virtually guarantee school improvement?

My colleagues and I eventually ended up in a mind-set something like this: the Components were not watertight elements and thus should not be positioned as a prescriptive formula to follow. Like sustainable school improvement itself, the *Components of School Excellence* was a "messy" mind-set with individual elements that were both interdependent and even somewhat concurrent. For example, most of those involved in the process agreed that school improvement should always follow a

- "why"
- "what"
- "how"

sequence of

- forming data-based consensus beliefs about the need to change and improve
- collectively deciding what the desired priority improvements needed to be and setting goals to meet them
- developing action plans and acting upon them, as well as regularly assessing progress against stated goals

But we conceded to ourselves that starting out with a clearly defined and shared vision was critical; that ongoing self-review, assessment, and adjustment as needed had to follow all other aspects of addressing the Components; and that Adopt Effective Instructional Practices might possibly be the single most significant component of school improvement to address.

Drawing upon its work with districts and schools across the country, the International Center has consistently encouraged the primacy of instruction in helping students to achieve and to reach their fullest potentials as individuals – wherever those capacities may ultimately lie. A shared vision of what the school needs to do and be is critical; curriculum matters; leadership is critical; physical space and organizational structures and procedures facilitate student achievement. But based on the successful schools we have partnered with and subsequently shared as models with others, we have witnessed - and urged upon the educators we partner with – the primacy of instruction over all else:

- As noted previously in this book, the Rigor/Relevance Framework™ is a conceptual framework based on the two related dimensions of higher standards and greater student achievement.
- Learning happens most easily and most effectively for most students when curriculum-instruction is/are applied and contextualized, i.e., in the C (Assimilation) and D (Adaptation) Quadrants of that construct.
- Conversely, learning occurs less often and least effectively for most students when curriculum-instruction is only recall of simple, unapplied knowledge or more complex thinking but still unapplied and for its own sake.
- Instruction is an art and a craft.
- Even the best teaching ideas don't work in every situation with every student.
- Every teacher needs a professional "toolkit" or repertoire of varied instructional strategies such as the 17 described in the International Center's Instructional Strategies: How to Teach for Rigor and Relevance workshops and publications.
- Each student and every human mind must be regarded as an integrated, interdependent combination of intellect, senses, emotions, knowledge, and skills.
- Learning solutions must derive from a systematic application of inputs from learners, crafted by the teacher's knowledge, empathy, and sensitivities.

103

- Instructional strategies should draw upon, but not be limited by, all available resources including technology, physical space, print resources, "real-world" experiences, game playing, kinesthetics, and teaching aids (as well as teaching aides).

In 1997, I wrote a book with the late Benedict Kruse titled *Education is NOT a Spectator Sport.* At that time, we made the case for an emphasis in the classroom on learning, not teaching. This was a subtle notion at the time, but one that is as true today as it was then.

The greatest difference between good schools and great schools is what happens in the classrooms. In great schools, you can truly see the difference. You can hear it and feel it as soon as you walk into the building, and it becomes strikingly apparent when you enter the classrooms. In the nation's most successful schools, students are actively engaged in the learning process. In less successful schools, it would appear to an objective observer that students come to school so they can watch their teachers work. However, we mustn't confuse teachers working with students learning: they are not the same thing.

Teaching does not assume learning. The processes are separate and, fortunately for advocates of sustainable school improvement, teaching and learning can be implemented independently of each other. Learning is measured by the acquisition of knowledge and the ability to apply that knowledge logically and purposefully to solve problems and gain further understandings.

Teaching, on the other hand, assumes control and dissemination of information – and assessment of that performance – to a group of students by a designated authority on the subject matter, the proverbial "sage on the stage." Teaching assumes that the knowledge will be received, processed, and retained, much like a download from a Web site or file server. However, unlike computers and computing devices, information download is not a given, and file storage for later retrieval and use is not guaranteed by such a process that involves human brains instead of digital memory. In fact, in teaching, there are frequent downlink malfunctions: the biological unit receptors do not receive, let alone internalize, the data transmitted.

At the risk of "crashing" this extended digital metaphor, let's examine some reasons. For one, information-flow is not an easily engineered process when human beings are involved. "Command prompts" do not always work as intended, and the receptors and intake and storage devices in people do not have to automatically accept the information sent. In other words, children have choice; computing devices do not. Teaching can happen independently of a successful download or transmission. Learning cannot, but requires active consent on the part of the learner.

Secondly, the intake and storage devices are neither all manufactured to spec nor always cross-platform compatible with the source devices. Unlike digital component parts, kids are individually all different. No two are the same. Moreover, many do not respond to the same stimuli, triggering processes, intake methods, or activation codes that we adults have internalized and, in some cases, been programmed to follow. Many of my audiences have heard me talk about intergenerational dissonance: that kids today are "wired differently" and respond to (frequently simultaneously and multiple source) stimuli in ways that baby boomer or even Gen X educators cannot, and in digital environments that were not even in Version 1.0 prototype when we toiled through textbooks, sound filmstrips, and chalk dust.

Lastly – although this comparison with human-devised computing devices could probably be extended – learners need to recognize purpose and value, not just data. Copying to a hard drive does not involve convincing the storage device that the information being saved is – or will be – useful. It does not involve prior knowledge, recognition, context, or connection with anything more than wires or wireless receptors and silicon chips. In contrast, acceptance of information and knowledge in the world of the learner – younger and older – needs engagement on several levels including:

- feeling safe, secure, and free to learn
- being healthy, rested, and nether hungry or distracted by factors outside the learning environment
- believing that someone cares about the learner as a

person and as a unique individual and wants her or him to be successful

- operating in an environment that is, while not necessarily dust-free and temperature-controlled, at least supportive, collaborative, and respectful of all involved
- seeing connections from what is being introduced to prior knowledge and experience
- recognizing value in and purpose for learning what is being taught
- at some level, being stimulated by the topic at hand – either the content itself, the interactions with other learners and learning coaches during the learning process, or the discovery process itself

In short, quality instruction recognizes the prerequisite of security, freedom from criticism, and student engagement. Whether seeing connections and value or experiencing a sense that the new learning is "cool" (that may be a stretch, but something at least not "lame" – to use the student vernacular), learning is dependent on students being engaged and taking responsibility for their own learning.

Yes, the operating instructions and set-up manual for human learners are more finicky and demanding than those followed to set up a new laptop, digital TV, or cell phone.

Education - in the sense of real learning - succeeds in direct proportion to the extent that each student is allowed to acquire the knowledge and skills being learned in his or her own way and at his or her own pace. Teaching – especially to a whole group in a standard, predetermined, and teacher-convenient fashion – exists independent of audience. Education may be an intended outcome but is all too frequently not a result for all but a few of the consumers.

How Brain Research Informs Instruction

In our ongoing work in identifying, observing, and analyzing instructional practices in some of the nation's most effective schools, we at the International Center were also working to understand the growing body of knowledge coming out of the explosion in brain research that was occurring across the country and around the world. One of the primary reasons for the explosions in brain research has been the increased capacity of imaging technology including CAT scans, PET scans, and MRIs. As we began to lay over what the schools were doing with their commonsense instructional practices with the growing body of brain research, it became increasingly apparent what was happening: their most successful teaching and learning practices were mirroring what sound brain research was telling us. Therefore, it became apparent to us that we - and all educators - needed to acquaint ourselves with the growing body of knowledge in brain research and then translate that knowledge into additional replicable practices to be used in their classrooms.

As a result, we have immersed ourselves in the last few years in the physiological underpinnings of how the human brain works and its impact on learning. Neurophysiologists and cognitive scientists - such as my esteemed colleague, International Center keynoter and consultant, neuropsychologist Dr. Paul D. Nussbaum of the University of Pittsburgh - remind us that the human brain is an even more remarkable computing device than we had imagined before we had the advantage of current brain research. As Paul has said so well:

> The single greatest and most miraculous part of you is your brain! There is no other system in our universe with the same complexity, efficiency, or capacity of the human brain. Sometimes I chuckle to hear others speak in awe of their laptop computer or the latest digital gadget. I wonder if those so inspired by their laptop have ever given serious consideration to the ultimate "wireless" and "portable" machine — the human brain.

Paul's insights into the brain have direct applications to student learning and the controllable variables that inform instruction.
  • Brain development and the creation of new learning are naturally occurring biological processes.

107

- Brain development is not "set" and therefore can be nurtured.
- A rich learning environment has a direct, positive impact on brain growth and "brain health."

He concludes that such capacity in the learning part of the brain is attributable to three primary factors: (1) socialization, (2) physical activity, and (3) mental stimulation.

> One goal you should have is to develop as many synaptic connections across your lifespan. Synaptic density (having many connections between brain cells) occurs as a result of an enriched environment.

Susan J. Kovalik is a nationally acclaimed education leader and associate of the International Center who has worked for decades with teachers and schools at The Center for Effective Learning in Seattle, Washington. This organization, which she founded and leads as president, has focused on identifying and making accessible to teachers direct connections between the cognitive sciences and classroom learning and instruction. Her resource kit, *How Brain Research Impacts Instruction,* published in cooperation with the International Center, describes how what we are discovering about brain structures and functions can be directly applied to classroom instructional practices and the K-12 learning environment. Susan's Highly Effective Teaching (HET) Model and Principles were developed to give educators, in her words, "greater understanding and appreciation of current brain research and its applications in education."

Susan's valued perspective as an educator with an abiding interest in brain science builds on the medical/scientific/human health care viewpoints of Dr. Nussbaum's and has informed my intuitive, but not nearly so learned, view of the critical importance of instruction. She writes:

> By providing a biological base one can better begin to develop a comprehensive view in relation to

curriculum development and instructional strategies needed to improve student learning and achievement.

Learning is the result of real, observable physiological growth in the brain that occurs as a result of sensory input and the processing, organizing, and pruning it promotes. This factor is the important issue in the great nature versus nurture debate about intelligence. It now appears that there is plenty of scientific evidence to establish the power of both. Genetics is not the immutable determiner of intelligence it was generally believed to be; although it sets parameters, it is experiences with high levels of sensory input that can significantly increase development of one's capacity. Indeed, it is through daily experiences that we either increase, stifle, or diminish intellectual, social, and/or emotional capacity.

If learning is the result of such physiological changes, then the question for teachers becomes: What should the classroom teacher do to maximize growth in the brain? The answers aren't mysterious or complicated yet they fly in the face of our traditional curricular tools and instructional processes.

The widely used HET Model describes five core "bodybrain-compatible" learning principles that apply brain research to instruction:
1. Intelligence is a function of experience.
2. Learning is an inseparable partnership between the brain and body.
3. There are multiple intelligences.
4. Learning is a two-step process:
   - The brain makes meaning through pattern seeking.
   - Most information we use is embedded in programs, planned sequences to accomplish a purpose or goal
5. Personality/temperament has an impact on learning.

HET's wisdom and practical applications mirror, and lend a well-reasoned and practicable scientific basis to, our own experiences in observing why and how some of the nation's most successful schools have put instruction first.

Rigor/Relevance Framework Applied to Instruction: Some Best Practices

Without repeating previously discussed content, let's briefly review the conceptual model of the Rigor/Relevance Framework, introduced in Chapter 2.

As described in an earlier section of this chapter, effective instruction is inventive, varied, applied, and engaging for students.

In many of the nation's highest performing schools, instruction is frequently in Quadrant B: Application and Quadrant D: Adaptation. When instruction is structured with these quadrants in mind, teachers are facilitators of the learning process. As teachers share information, students are encouraged

Rigor/Relevance Framework™

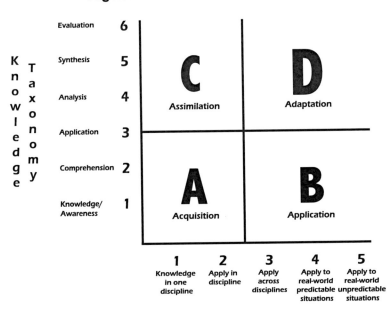

Application Model

to ask: "When will I ever use what you are teaching me today?" And when one observes the projects that the students are engaged in, it is apparent that they are based in the real world. The students' active involvement in applying the academic skills they are learning is evident.

In other high-performing schools, technology is effectively exploited in both teacher-enabling and student-centered ways. Sometimes, as in the case of Greenwood High School in Bowling Green, KY, that uses electronic white boards to teach students and share favorite lessons and data with colleagues, technology is used to help teachers do a better job of teaching in different and more collaborative ways. In many other successful schools, technology is used to teach in *new* ways. Widely used, research-based, and effectiveness-proven computer-managed instructional programs such as Scholastic's *READ 180* and JRL Enterprises' I CAN Learn Mathematics programs actively engage students at all levels in learning, exploring, and developing skills on an individualized and personalized basis and have helped many thousands of students to achieve at higher levels than students being taught in more traditional ways.

At many other high-performing schools that the International Center has been honored to work with, students are required to take the knowledge presented and apply it in multiple ways. The academics taught in math, science, and English language arts are applied daily in other disciplines such as the arts, career and technical education, health, and physical education. This requires schools to have teachers working in interdisciplinary teams and to engage in careful instructional planning on a daily, weekly, and annual basis. Teachers at Kennesaw Mountain High School in Kennesaw, Georgia, use the Picasso software program to design and share lessons that not only address state standards, but also apply academic standards within, beyond, and across academic disciplines. For example, in Algebra 1 students make recommendations to their parents and grandparents about whether to accept Social Security payments beginning at age 62 or 65.

Many of the schools that have impressed us instructionally are further challenged with large populations of students who are English language learners, qualify for free-and-reduced lunch programs, or are in IEPs. One such school is Roy W. Martin Middle School in Las Vegas. Only 14 percent of Martin's diverse student population make up the white subgroup; 71 percent are Hispanic. Eleven percent of students have IEPs, 28 percent are designated limited English proficient, and 46 percent qualify for the free-and-reduced lunch program. The school has learning improvement teams, an active Parent Advisory Council, and extensive emphasis on literacy improvement and applied communications using inventive strategies such as Breakfast with Books, intercultural awareness, an academic-based summer camp, and community service programs. It also has an impressive partnership with UNLV that provides volunteer in-class tutors who devote 19 hours a week to working with students.

The teaching of academics through multiple disciplines and creating a supportive and nurturing, no-risk environment for instruction and learning are themes that are consistent with all we have learned in recent years about brain research. The more pathways we create for students around essential skills and knowledge, the more connections they will make that enable them to both master the content and (equally, if not more importantly) retain and use it in multiple ways once they leave school. As our friend and partner Susan Kovalik of Center for Effective Learning likes to remind the teachers she coaches: "Grow those dendrites!"

Focusing instruction in Quadrants B and D and addressing the needs of individual learners enhances achievement – both to help students "pass the test" and to enable them to become lifelong learners prepared to succeed in the changing landscape of the 21st century.

Why Relationships Underpin Instruction and Learning

Since our beginnings, the International Center's core belief has been that what *all* students need to succeed in the 21st century is an education based on curriculum and instruction that are both academically rigorous and relevant to the real world. As schools and teachers struggle to cope with new accountability requirements, it is clear we cannot achieve better results by following the same-old, same-old practices, or even by simply working harder at those previously less-than-effective approaches. Different results require different solutions.

While rigor and relevance are of paramount importance, we are increasingly seeing a need for a third "R" – relationships. This alliterative triplet is more than a clever twist on the traditional 3Rs of reading, 'ritin', and 'rithmetic. It reflects the realization that relationships are of critical importance to the learning process.

Relationships are not a new standard; they are a way to improve learning and are critical components of high achievement. Having positive relationships will not, by itself, create high levels of student achievement. Relationships are critically important, however, because they are linked with and complement – and in some ways, even nurture - rigor and relevance.

There are four dimensions of relationships that are important in schools:

- Learning relationships among and between students are essential for support in the learning process. They are formed from a combination of relationships with parents, administrators, nonteaching staff, and teachers.
- Staff relationships are the links among teachers, support staff, and administrators that influence teaching, support functions, staff retention and development, and school decisions and problem solving.
- Professional relationships are the relationships each educator creates and maintains to learn and develop in her or his profession. This includes groups and individual mentors from whom an educator learns as well as those who provide a supportive environment within the profession. This group often extends beyond the school or district where an educator is employed, such as subject-specialist organizations and educator professional organizations such as the International Center.
- Community relationships are the relationships that the school as an organization forges with parents, business leaders, and community leaders.

As the International Center has examined some of the country's most successful high schools, what has become clear is that a key element of their success is a deliberate nurturing of relationships among students and staff. This is true in schools that have succeeded despite the challenges of poverty, diversity, and mobility. In these schools, students feel the staff genuinely cares about them and encourages them to achieve at higher levels. Experience in working with these schools indicates that when student expectations are raised, there is also a need to focus on the quality of relationships and support for students. If positive relationships are not high, students will not respond as well to higher expectations.

One of the barriers to higher achievement most frequently cited by administrators and teachers is that students lack motivation to learn what is being taught. One could also define this problem as a lack of student involvement in their own learning, or disengagement. On third-party studies and student opinion surveys, many students consistently report that they do not work as hard as they are capable of:

- if they cannot see the relevance of what they are learning
- if they perceive that no one in the school cares if they succeed or take a direct interest in them personally

Students often ask the question, "Why do I need to learn this?" but receive an inadequate answer. They need to see what is truly important for them to learn, and they need to know that adults and peers care whether they learn. That means teachers need to provide a relevant contextual base and a supportive environment for the knowledge and skills they teach. Education is meaningless when it is reduced to an unending list of content topics for which the student quickly learns the facts, takes the test, and then forgets the facts - and gets the distinct sense that no one really expects better from them or cares.

Rigorous and relevant instruction presents projects and problems in a defined context, which makes it more likely that students will make the connections and see the value of what they are learning. When this happens, rigor naturally follows. Strong relationships are essential to creating the sense of value in what is to be learned that allows completing rigorous work successfully. Students are also more likely to make a personal commitment to engage in their own rigorous learning when they know teachers, parents, and other students actually care about how well they do. They are willing to continue making an investment when they are encouraged, supported, and assisted, much in the same way that a personal trainer or coach might work with an athlete, musician, or artist who lacks the will or confidence to continue. For students to engage fully in challenging learning, they require increased levels of support from the people – adults and peers — around them.

In addition to relationships around the student as learner, relationships among staff are also important. In model schools, it is evident that staff members support each other and learn from one another. In these schools, teachers enjoy their work and perform as a team, sharing the burden of effective teaching. Good leaders inspire others and, in the process, develop positive relationships with and among staff. Likewise, good teachers break down student isolation and facilitate learning by providing a strong supportive environment for students.

Positive relationships occur in many schools. The question is whether, in the process of school improvement, we can elevate relationships from a "nice-to-have-but-not-requisite" characteristic we observe to a dimension of a school that we can measure, set goals around, plan for, and systematically improve. The International Center has developed a Relationship Framework that enables us to quantify relationships. The framework describes seven levels of relationships.

- Level 0: Isolation – This indicates a lack of any positive relationships.
- Level 1: Known – A person must know someone before a relationship is formed, so this is the first step in getting to know someone. This step includes learning about another person's family and his or her likes and dislikes, aspirations, and learning style.
- Level 2: Receptive – Showing you are interested and genuinely care about developing a relationship comes

from frequent contact in multiple settings and from taking an active interest in someone.

- Level 3: Reactive – At this level, one person receives guidance or support from another. This relationship yields emotional support or cognitive information.
- Level 4: Proactive – Partners at this stage share a proactive commitment to do more than assist when needed; they take an active interest in supporting the other person. They have moved beyond simply reacting to the other person.
- Level 5: Sustained – Positive support is balanced from all family members, peers, and teachers. This relationship, which endures over a long period of time, is the level that effective parents have with their children.
- Level 6: Mutually Beneficial – While occurring rarely in education, this level finds both parties contributing support to each other for an extended period of time. A healthy, happy, long-term marriage is a good example of a mutually beneficial relationship.

The Relationship Framework is useful because it helps teachers understand that there are degrees of relationships. When they think about their relationships with students, teachers can use the framework to apply a qualitative measure to the relationships they make and work hard to secure. This qualitative measure helps them consider their current levels and allows them to decide if they wish to make changes to improve those relationships. When relationships are simply categorized as "good" or "bad," there is no need for change. If the relationship is "bad," it is easy to become defensive, blame the other party, or simply accept things as they are. A leveled framework has a different effect on teachers. Even a poor relationship offers some positive aspects upon which to build and improve. And for "good" relationships, the framework indicates the potential for growth and further improvement. In this scenario, all administrators and teachers need to work on improving relationships regardless of the current level of success.

How Do You Make Meaningful Instructional Improvement Happen?

Instructional improvement in reading, writing, mathematics, science, social studies, or any other discipline requires individualized solutions for schools and districts. However, administrators and teachers do not have to invent it from scratch or manage the process single-handedly. Research-based reading intervention models, tools, and metrics are available. Most of these resources have data-based, quantified, and proof statements that attest to their effectiveness.

A good first step in answering *how* to bring about change is to take a look at what model schools have done and are doing. To help schools learn from other schools' successes, the International Center has sought out and shared models and best practices through the Successful Practices Network.

Second, we have found that schools that establish school or districtwide literacy plans tend to have greater success. Many successful schools start with a commitment to literacy and then create a comprehensive plan to address identified needs using a systematic and inclusive approach. In addition, these schools have realized that certain key steps in devising and implementing such a strategy improve the odds for success. Some of the case studies in Chapter 8 highlight successful strategies schools have used to accomplish this initiative.

Once an instructional improvement plan is developed, you can move to the third step: defining specific steps in the plan. Plan specifics will vary from situation to situation as will the order of implementation, but the planning process typically requires leaders to do the following:

- Confront the issue and reach consensus that there is a need for change, which requires a collaborative effort.
- Be inclusive in seeking input. Involve teachers, administrators, parents, students, and community partners in the process.
- Don't expect every participant to be committed 100 percent. Some participants will embrace and champion the issue; some will help; and some will resist.

- Research and study relevant tools, resources, models, and best practices.
- Use data (as discussed in Chapter 2) to define the problem and to set measurable goals to help participants picture what success will look like.
- Adopt common language, assessments, and rubrics. This includes conversing with all parties involved to ensure consistent communication.
- Nurture the sense that every teacher is a master teacher and that instructional challenges are the responsibility of every teacher in the school
- Brainstorm solutions, select strategies that will guide the planning process, and devise specific plans that can be implemented.
- Be flexible regarding changes that may need to be made to the master schedule, the school day, length of classes, and use of time during, before, and after school.
- Seek solutions that address all aspects of reading and literacy – phonics, word recognition, fluency, vocabulary, and comprehension – and math – numeracy, computation, measurement, spatial awareness, statistics and probability, quantitative literacy and problem solving – and then offer individualized learning tools that employ the most time-tested instructional strategies and latest instructional technologies to engage students.
- Use a universal framework with common vocabulary and standard measurement tools to establish quantifiable yardsticks to talk about curriculum standards and instruction.
- Document plans and integrate them into existing curriculum, instruction, and assessment guidelines. Assign responsibilities and establish timeframes.
- Launch the initiative with fanfare. Include a communications plan and a time frame. Keep the initiative front and center in the minds of staff and students.
- Review progress regularly. A manageable, teacher-friendly, real-time tracking component and student

progress management component are essential. Share successes and measure progress with supportive data. Offer rewards whenever possible.

- Adjust the plan as needed and recognize that success will not happen overnight. Make sure both staff and leaders understand they are committing to a long-term plan.
- Provide ongoing professional development to support the teaching staff. Consider using a provider of instructional resources and tools to do professional development. Some providers offer online training and time-of-use assistance for teachers.
- Establish a cross-curricular instructional improvement team to support the initiative, and provide continuing training and support.

The fourth step in the process is to adopt a measurement tool to help define the extent of the issues and to inform planning, as well as quality instructional tools to address the issues identified. For example, the Lexile Framework for Reading is an excellent tool for this as it allows schools and teachers to match any reader with reading material of an appropriate readability level. The framework also provides a common rubric for assessing, discussing, comparing, and forecasting reading ability and readability. Many states are now using the Lexile Framework to evaluate commercially published instructional materials. Most of the major commercial assessment and testing services publishers can provide student data measured in Lexiles.

The fifth and final step in this planning process is the selection and implementation of research-based intervention programs for students who are disengaged or academically challenged. I have seen many of the schools that we work with deploy to good advantage Scholastic's *READ 180*, a comprehensive reading intervention program that directly addresses individual needs through adaptive and instructional software, high-interest leveled literature, and direct instruction in reading and writing skills. The program incorporates six crucial elements of reading intervention and has been successfully deployed by hundreds of schools across the country.

Addressing Instruction and Achievement
for Special Education Students

I would be remiss – professionally and personally – in not making particular mention of how instruction applies to our students with special needs.

The debate about the effects of *No Child Left Behind* on students with disabilities typically involves three different viewpoints:

- Stay the course and tough it out.
- Keep special education students in the accountability system, but give them different tests and hold them to different standards.
- Take the students out of the NCLB accountability system because it is unreasonable and unfair to expect that these students will perform at the same level as other students.

The evolution of accountability for education programs for students with disabilities has slowly inched its way from accountability for process and procedure to accountability for educational performance. NCLB has presented an unprecedented dilemma for special education programs. For its first 22 years, special education as we know it today was a prescriptive, federally driven program; procedural compliance was the rule. Concern for access and protections, which provided the momentum behind the original 1975 *Individuals with Disabilities Education Act,* known then as the *Education for All Handicapped Children Act* (PL 94–142), dominated special education accountability. Many educators griped about this, but grudgingly attempted to comply with the complicated and ever-growing maze of requirements.

This direction began to change as the movement to raise standards took hold in the mid-1990s. Policymakers were confronted with the proposition that, if they were to raise standards and improve learning results, they could not choose which students would be affected; it would have to be all students. At the same time, organizations such as the Education Trust published research that exposed enormous "achievement gaps" between certain subgroups of students and the general student population. Policymakers and some researchers began to question why these groups were so far behind.

The subgroup that has recently caused the most consternation and concern is the special education population. Why are educators so conflicted over academic expectations for this group of students? One reason is that, historically, expectations for this population were shaped during a time when the students in special education were a homogeneous group. This group has become increasingly diverse in type of disability, with a growing percentage of school enrollment being classified as needing special education services. The driving force behind the landmark 1975 legislation had been parents of children with mental retardation or multiple disabilities, while the population receiving special education in 1995 was primarily identified as learning disabled, emotionally disturbed, and speech impaired. The population had changed significantly, and expectations did not keep pace.

In 1997, with the reauthorization of the *Individuals with Disabilities Education Act* (IDEA), special education accountability crossed the magic line from process to educational performance. Most educators cheered this moment: finally, access to the general education curriculum was a primary focus for special needs students. Accountability systems were to include them, and reports of their performance were to be as routine as all other reports on student performance. After all these years, students with disabilities had finally been recognized as a group whose members, in many if not most cases, could and should be able to meet the requirements of state standards. As the reauthorization made clear, special education should be considered a service rather than a place where students are sent. States and local districts began to show progress in performance for students receiving special education services. This was an exciting time for those of us involved at the state and local levels.

Then along came NCLB, and how quickly the attitudes of some educators changed! The policies and adequate yearly progress (AYP) provisions designed to implement NCLB have created dilemmas regarding accountability that even the most ardent supporters of the effort to help students with disabilities meet high standards are finding troublesome. "AYP" has supplanted "IEP" (individual education plan) as the acronym most used in discussions among special educators.

In the view of the International Center, the problem as we see it is not with the *intent* of the AYP provision but with the *design* of its implementation for this population. To begin with, the idea of setting a hard-and-fast percentage of students who could be considered for an alternative assessment is flawed. In an ideal world, that might be desirable. But in the real world, a uniform percentage cannot be expected to be right for each district and every state.

Another problem is the requirement that AYP rules be applied in the same way to special education students as to the general education population. The fact is that only recently have many of these students been exposed to the full general education curriculum on a regular basis. Moreover, special education services are still undergoing realignment as the expectation to have more effective instructional strategies and programs in place grows nationwide.

Today, as AYP results are reported, educators have been sounding the alarm that it is the special education students who are causing their schools to be considered in need of improvement, which is unfair to schools. This reaction could place the onus for achievement on the special education students, and we could end up with a scenario in which school administrators and others point to special education students as the reason their otherwise "good school" is not meeting its annual progress goals. It appears that NCLB has exposed an issue concerning the expectations of educators that was hidden below the surface of the IDEA requirements. While many educators believed it was acceptable to begin to account for the educational performance of these students, they find it less acceptable to be held accountable for continuous improvement for these results.

Finally, but certainly not least worthy of consideration, is the issue of "highly qualified teachers," which has raised a concern among those responsible for implementing NCLB. Some educators feel it is unrealistic to expect special education teachers also to be qualified to teach academic subjects. The concern is that this will drive even more teachers out of the field or result in students being placed inappropriately in general education classrooms in order to be taught by "qualified" teachers.

Are these perhaps the wrong concerns? Shouldn't we be more concerned about the student who may be capable of mastering a curriculum based on high standards but who, by virtue of being classified as needing special education services, is being taught by a teacher who does not have the knowledge to teach, for example, biology? We all know there are special education students in this situation today, although perhaps not as many as in the past. But particularly in many large and poor districts, this is still the case for a significant number of students.

There are strategies that can be put in place to address these challenges and make good on the intentions of the legislation to ensure that special education services are provided within the context of high-quality instruction. We must avoid the possibility of students with disabilities once again being set aside from the world of high expectations and rigorous curricula that must be available to all students if they are to be competitive, independent, and capable of participating fully in this complex world in which we live.

Special education and NCLB can co-exist, and students with disabilities can benefit from a law that clearly has placed the spotlight on the significant achievement gap that exists between certain groups of students in this country. We cannot retreat to a position that continues the tradition of low expectations for students receiving special education services. On the other hand, we cannot expect dramatic improvement in educational performance from many of these students until instructional programs are realigned to give them the supports and opportunities that will allow them to succeed. A steady path to increased expectations and insistence on continuous improvement in educational performance define the prudent way to proceed.

CHAPTER SIX

Form Follows Function:

Addressing Organizational Structures

We're all familiar with the saying that "form follows function." By the same token, instruction should drive structure, rather than structure driving instruction.

Too often, a school begins its reform initiative by looking at such organizational structures as length of school year, school calendar, bell schedules, or schools-within-schools. Based on the International Center's work with the nation's highest performing schools, I strongly discourage this approach. Reform initiatives should be built around the successful practices that are being used at the classroom level. After all, it is better and more productive to play to one's strengths than to follow the latest popular trend.

We have discussed the importance of creating multiple pathways to learning. Such actions can be taken in any organizational structure that exists in schools today. When such integration is proposed, typically you will find that about one-third of the staff is excited and wants to do it immediately. Another third is more cautious, asking for support and proof that it will work. The final third basically says, "No way will you do anything to mess up the lesson plan I've been using since 1980!"

If you move too quickly on organizational issues, you require the entire faculty and staff to change. That will cause that uncooperative third to dig in its heels against many reform initiatives. If, however, you begin with instruction rather than structure, you will find that the uncooperative third will not be as threatened and, in fact, may simply ignore your reform efforts. The supportive third will enthusiastically begin to make appropriate changes to instruction as long as leadership provides necessary assistance and resources. As the supportive third changes and experiences success, the hesitant third will watch and then attempt to emulate the successes of the supportive third. And, not requiring all staff members to comply silences the resistant third, which allows the cautious third to try the initiative without hearing negative talk. We find that by the third to fifth year, many in the uncooperative third do begin to accept change.

Once the majority of staff is on board and there are changes happening in classrooms, you are truly ready to deal with the structural or organizational changes. You are ready to explore strategies such as small learning communities, block scheduling, schools-within-schools, academies, and so forth. Success with these strategies is more likely to put everyone on the same page, working toward the common goal.

Size Matters: Small Learning Communities

Studies show that academic performance improves for many students when they are taught in a magnet school or theme academy setting. Some districts use schools-within-schools or alternative schools to create these more focused learning communities. But whatever structure is used, small learning communities are frequently organized around a theme or career area. Theme- or career-focused small learning communities are better able to focus on individual students' needs. Carefully planned instruction, aligned with academic standards and taught in a context that interests students, leads to greater relevance of instruction. More relevant instruction increases student interest and deepens learning through application. Students are better able to retain skills and knowledge and to demonstrate proficiency in those skills at a later time.

Small learning communities may differ in size or structure, but they often share essential elements and traits that support their success. A smaller setting on its own does not automatically improve teaching and learning, but it does provide the right conditions and settings for high-quality instruction and student achievement. Successful small learning communities typically involve a small body of students taught by the same group of teachers. These communities often use designated physical space and focus on a common instructional theme. Other key elements include giving the communities enough authority to make their own decisions; creating an identity that students and teachers willingly embrace; developing personal relationships among teachers and students; an instructional focus on student achievement; and accountability by all parties involved. In addition, small learning communities may employ a number of similar strategies, including:

- alternative scheduling that allow teachers to develop lessons to meet student learning needs and to provide longer instructional blocks of time, thus allowing community and business representatives to better support learning during the school day
- teacher advisory systems in which teachers advise small groups of students and serve as an extension of the guidance program
- adult advocacy systems, similar to the teacher advisory system, in which an adult from the community is assigned students to whom he or she provides personal, professional, and academic guidance
- recognizing and highly valuing parent outreach as a essential element in ensuring that students set and achieve goals
- academic teams that share students and that are organized across departments to help teachers better focus on the "whole" student; teams are responsible for curriculum, instruction, and even scheduling decisions

- freshman transition activities that focus on easing the move from middle school to high school by providing extra support services for all students and helping to identify those who need additional help to succeed in high school

School-Within-a-School

This is an autonomous program situated within a larger school facility. Students take all their classes in the school-within-the-school, and all of a teacher's classes are assigned here. This model allows a high degree of personalization and student support because it encourages sustained relationships among students and teachers. Such programs also provide the flexibility for developing a unique culture and program of studies.

Academies

Academies are usually a school-within-a-school that is designed around an occupational or arts theme. Students experience many real-world applications of learning and participate in work-based learning programs. School-to-work elements are immersed in the academic programs of students in this structure. The academy consists of a group of students who stay with the same teachers for two to four years, resulting in a personalized and supportive learning environment. The course of study provides high academic standards that are integrated within career and technical education or arts education. A key component of academies is partnerships with businesses that provide real-world support and feedback.

Houses

Houses allow for students in a large school to be divided into smaller groups, which may include members of the same grade or several grades. Students take and teachers teach most (but not all) of their classes within the house. The house plan provides a higher degree of personalization and stronger teacher-student relationships than a traditional school structure. However, unlike a school-within-a-school, a house structure is not autonomous from the hosting school or its administrators; it may not even have a dedicated physical space for the house plan.

Freshman Academy/House

A variation on the house plan, freshman academies/houses allow incoming freshmen to slowly transition into the full high school experience.

Magnet Schools

These schools are built around a central theme or area, such as the arts or technology. As the name implies, a magnet school "attracts" students from across the district who are interested in the theme. A magnet school may be located in its own building or it may be contained within a larger school. Students in a magnet school take their core specialty courses together, but they may join non-magnet students for courses outside their core focus.

Reinventing High School

While small learning communities address specific needs of certain populations, the fact is that most often, the entire high school system needs to be revised. For example, 9th grade is typically the entry point to high school, serving as the indoctrination into a culture of high expectations and new social experiences. The struggle to improve the performance of high school students begins with their entrance in 9th grade and continues throughout their final years in the public school system. When 9th graders are not successful academically, which is true for 30 percent to 40 percent of freshmen, there is a domino effect up through graduation, if they do, in fact, graduate. High schools that make a commitment to 9th grade improvements, such as through freshman academies or houses, find that that poises students to succeed not just in their transitional year, but throughout high school and beyond.

High schools today need to be reinvented to keep pace with changes in society. Students and adults must continually learn new things. Moreover, some of the skills we teach and use today will soon be as outdated as the skills once needed to operate a typewriter or a slide rule. Technological change is inevitable, and schools need to be ready to deal with it. We talked at length about four mega-trends facing American culture in Chapter 1. Most schools still follow an agrarian calendar and were designed for the industrial age, not the digital age. In many districts, schools are not designed to deal with today's technology or with the global, media-driven pace. They are not designed to address equity issues facing modern education. These schools still operate under rules and regulations designed for a time that has passed.

Today's students must work harder, faster, and smarter than their parents did in order to enjoy success as adults. Schools need to reinvent themselves to prepare students for the demands of the future; flexibility and adaptability is required.

Successful schools tend to create systems that are future-focused. The goal is to teach students how to think, not simply to tell them what to know. These schools know that students need to learn to apply high levels of cognitive knowledge to unpredictable situations in the real world; instruction must be rigorous and relevant and it must focus on preparing students with a Quadrant D: Adaptation skill set (see chapter 2). This means applying academic rigor in open-ended ways relevant to the new millennium.

The International Center has maintained for many years that relevance is critical if we want to move students to rigor. Relevance can help create the conditions and motivation needed for students to make a personal investment in rigorous work for optimal learning. Simply put, students invest more of themselves, work harder, and learn better when a topic is connected to something they already know about or in which they have an interest.

Rigor and relevance are critical to student success, but they are not sufficient alone. They must be linked with relationships. The level of rigor tends to increase as the degree of relevance and the quality of relationships improve. Rigor requires students to make a substantial personal investment in their own learning. Students involved in rigorous learning are deeply engaged in thought, critical analysis, research, problem solving, reflection, and synthesis. They exercise their cognitive abilities to the maximum level when they are engaged.

Likewise, strong relationships are critical to academic success. Relationships are important because students are more likely to engage in rigorous learning when they know teachers, parents, and peers really care about how well they do. They are willing to keep trying when they are connected, encouraged, supported, and assisted.

Students with Specialized Learning Needs

Of particular importance across all grades is addressing the needs of students with specialized learning requirements. Academic success for public school students requires that educators be committed to and accountable for providing *all* students with a rigorous and relevant curriculum and instruction that is:
- based on strong relationships
- meets prescribed state standards
- complies with federal mandates for inclusion

Reading proficiency and fluency in mathematics have historically been valued as fundamental enabling competencies for achieving academic success. But for an increasing number of struggling or disengaged learners, achieving these competencies is a daily challenge. For these students, learning can be compromised by a variety of stressors, such as poverty, nutrition, health issues, the language spoken in the home, unstable families, peer pressure, bullying, substance abuse, organizational abilities, oral and written comprehension abilities, and other challenges.

All students – particularly those who are struggling and/or disengaged – need adaptations and accommodations for at least one of these stressors. Otherwise, they cannot maintain or increase the pace and effectiveness of their learning. Changes in the physical learning environment directly correlate to improvements in student achievement. Such changes help create a positive and supportive learning environment, which may help reduce the effects of life or situational stressors and lead to improved performance. Of course, creating the optimal educational setting requires design excellence: creative programming, planning, design, and landscape architecture of the learning environment. Let's consider the needs and appropriate physical space responses for several categories of struggling learners.

English Language Learners

For students who come from homes where English is rarely, if ever, spoken, being exposed to clearly spoken English in the classroom is critical. However, these children often face a variety of challenges when it comes to actually being able to hear in a classroom. For these students – and for many others – the quality of the acoustical environment is the most important quality that influences learning. A sound enhancement system helps these learners understand a teacher's calm, non-directional voice at normal sound levels. Combining a sound system with PowerPoint presentations and other equipment in a high-tech classroom has been proven to significantly increase achievement for ELL students.

Students With Disabilities

This group includes students with a diversity of physical, emotional and/or intellectual disorders that impair academic success. Students with disabilities learn in different ways and often require specific instructional aids and the use of a variety of learning strategies. The key to providing an optimum learning environment for these students is a rigorous analysis of the specific disorders and accompanying behaviors. Solutions may include low student-teacher ratios, cushioned flooring, use of primary colors, dimmer lighting, quieter classroom settings, or combinations of these strategies.

Economically Disadvantaged Learners

The cultural and economic diversity among learners in American schools today represents an immense challenge for the educational system. Economically disadvantage learners are highly linked to minority learners, and these students often come to school with fewer skills and facing more risk factors than children from other cultural groups. School often provides a safe haven from the turmoil and hardship of their lives outside the classroom. Support can be provided through health, nutrition, and social services programs; after-school programs; encouraging parental engagement with the school; and displays that recognize the cultural identities of all students.

Disengaged Learners

Students who struggle may lose interest in school and become disillusioned and disruptive; many eventually drop out of school. Many disengaged learners are average learners who are not as actively involved in the education system and who often cannot see how the subjects they are learning are relevant to their non-school lives. Disengaged learners may have a variety of personal challenges along with some of the other factors mentioned previously. A fundamental response to disengaged learners is to empower them by acknowledging that learning is the primary purpose of the school. For many disengaged learners, schools emit an institutional image that minimizes the individual. To counter this perception, schools may find it best to take an architectural approach to provide a variety of classroom shapes and sizes; large common spaces, such as auditoriums and dining areas, to encourage circulation and interaction; and gathering spots along hallways.

Beyond the physical space needs for challenged learners, there is a need for a well-designed learning environment that supports the rigorous and relevant learning of the academic environment. Creative and thoughtful design can help address the needs of struggling learners by providing positive support, stimulating the senses, and reducing stress.

Moving in the Right Direction: Steps Toward Change

Schools typically progress through three consecutive stages of change to achieve high academic standards for all students. These stages involve:

- convincing educators, parents, and members of the community why the school needs to change

- using good data to determine what the school's educational vision is, what needs to change, what will be taught, and how instruction will be organized
- Determining how to change the school, including creating a strategic collaborative plan and developing an understanding about the basics of managing change

Unfortunately, many schools take the reverse approach. They decide on what their solution will be before they have really defined the problem or identified the true needs. Regrettably, unless school staff and other stakeholders understand why change is needed, the effort is often doomed. Unless the problem has been acknowledged and agreed upon, suggestions about how to implement change are likely to be rejected or to be ineffective if implemented. We discussed the need to inform decisions using data in Chapter 2.

By examining successful schools, we see their leaders and their stakeholders often share an awareness of the economic and human reasons why education programs must change. They then use this shared knowledge to develop a student-focused vision. Their common focus helps them identify what changes will be needed (see Chapter 3).

Many successful high schools came to the conclusion on their own that their curricula were overcrowded. They used data to make hard decisions about what is essential for students to know versus what is nice to know; they figured out what should be taken off the table (see Chapter 4). Of all the critical areas of competency schools must maintain, literacy is first on the list. Literacy includes the need for students to be able to read, write, speak, listen, and observe well if they are to be effective lifelong learners. Writing is a key enabling skill as well. Successful schools are committed to teaching writing across disciplines and to teaching reading across the curriculum in all grades.

Beyond the basics, the real challenge in changing high schools is breaking free of traditions and assumptions that have become standard operating procedures in many of our schools. Those traditions include students having summers off, 45-minute class periods, and all courses lasting the same number of weeks.

We should challenge all decisions based on such traditions as "optimal class sizes." While deeply ingrained in our system, these traditions are not based on research that shows the most effective, efficient ways to education our children. After we challenge these assumptions, we must change the ones that are not aligned with a school's vision or students' needs.

As noted in our discussion of effective leadership in Chapter 3, change leaders in high-performing schools look at the process of how to change quite differently than do leaders in most other schools. Change leaders are willing to take risks, because they believe that not being willing to change is the worst possible choice. They understand that playing it safe is actually more dangerous than taking a risk, so they take control and push for solutions.

High-performing schools take an honest approach to communicating expectations. They help everyone understand that their plans are not perfect; in fact, there is no perfect model for change. These leaders know any plan will need constant adjustment and evaluation, so they let stakeholders know up front what they should anticipate as the plan evolves.

While improvement plans are designed to address student needs, they are also designed to play to the strengths of the community, students, faculty, and the school itself. Many reform campaigns spend too much time trying to figure out how to compensate for weaknesses; change becomes more difficult when schools focus on what is most problematic. A better approach is to capitalize on strengths. Focusing on positives energizes people and everyone is able to move ahead, even with an imperfect solution.

In 2004, the International Center partnered with the Council of Chief State School Officers on an initiative designed to provide policymakers and school districts with potential solutions to improving secondary education. That initiative, *Bringing Best Practices to Scale*, identified and studied high schools that have been most successful at providing all their students with a rigorous and relevant education. The 30 rural, urban, and suburban high schools included in the study provided great insight into how American high schools can help all students complete an academically rigorous and relevant curriculum.

While the study found no single formula for a successful high school, certain characteristics were consistent across those schools. If thoughtfully applied, these characteristics hold true for schools wishing to emulate the successes of the high performing schools included in the study.

- Instruction is focused around students' interests, learning styles, and aptitudes through a variety of small learning community approaches. Academies are the mostly commonly used approach.

- Administrators and teachers show unrelenting commitment to excellence for all students, and there is a particular emphasis on literacy across the curriculum. Educators at these schools recognized that a wide variety of delivery and support systems must be in place to enable students to achieve their potential.

- There is an intense focus on data use at the classroom level to make daily instructional decisions for individual students. Only essential data is collected, and that information is also communicated regularly to students, parents, and other stakeholders.

- Extraordinary resources and attention are committed to 9th graders. High-performing schools analyze individual academic levels as students entered ninth grade. Students who do not have adequate academic skills to succeed are enrolled in enrichment programs rather than traditional remediation programs, which have often shown limited success in improving performance. Ninth grade in the study schools looked dramatically different from the same grade in other schools.

- The final year of school looks dramatically different in successful high schools, with a particularly rigorous and relevant curriculum for 12th graders. When the curriculum is rigorous and relevant, students often complete most of the normal high school curriculum by grade 11, allowing grade 12 to be used as an "advanced placement" year. Through strong articulation with higher education, many of students are able to earn up to 30 college credits by the time they graduate from high school.

- A high-quality curriculum and instruction focuses on rigor, relevance, relationships, and reflective thought.
- Schools are run by solid and dedicated leaders who have solid skills, are well focused, and stay in the position long enough to sustain change within the school.
- Relationships drive guiding principles such as respect, adaptability, loyalty, courage, compassion, honesty, and perseverance.
- Professional development is sustained and supported for teachers and is guided by the same principles as quality education for students: it is teacher-centric, rigorous, relevant, and collaborative.

These defining characteristics can serve as guides to ensure rigorous, relevant instruction to help all students acquire the knowledge and skills needed to succeed in today's complex, technology-oriented society.

A key component to the success of these high schools is the amount of attention placed on successfully integrating incoming freshmen into their new environment. By the end of 9th grade, these students have typically made dramatic improvements in basic skills, enabling them to complete a normal high school curriculum. They have also been introduced to the culture of high expectations and caring adults. In fact, when grade 9 is used for enrichment, the normal four-year high school curriculum can be collapsed into the three years of grades 10 to 12. This can be done in most high schools because the senior year has a limited number of required courses. Furthermore, students often do not have a full slate of required courses in grade 11. Therefore, teachers may use the small learning community theme to teach academics. In effect, these schools trade off elective courses for the election of a thematic approach to teaching academics. In addition, upper-class students serve as mentors to incoming students; older students model expected behavior, provide ongoing guidance and, in many cases, tutor at-risk freshmen.

The model high schools in our study demonstrated the importance of building a culture of high academic expectations for all students, a tradition of continuous improvement, powerful structures of teaching and learning, collaborative leadership, and student support.

As other schools begin to make changes, they must continually analyze how they are doing. Along the way, they must revamp, refine and, when necessary, redirect the decisions and plans in place. The error is not in taking risks and making mistakes. For schools that attempt change, the error is not learning from missteps and not taking appropriate action. For schools that are complacent, the error is in not trying at all.

CHAPTER SEVEN

Paying Attention:

Monitoring Student Progress

Like it or not, testing is a new staple in American education. And for those who do not like testing programs, my only suggestion is very simple: get over it. Testing is part of our lives now, and tests are here to stay.

The *No Child Left Behind of 2001* (NCLB) showed a deep bipartisan commitment to the need for improving student performance in this country. Regardless of what happens to NCLB in the future, one thing is clear: state tests are not going away. Therefore, we need to make sure our students do well on them to ensure their individual success as well that of our nation.

Once again, let's look at the Rigor/Relevance Framework. We know that state tests simply measure Quadrant A: Acquisition learning and skills. I think we can all agree that, since they only look at Quadrant A, state tests are not adequate to meet all of our needs, although they are essential for measuring student progress. We know that success in life requires mastery of Quadrant C: Assimilation, plus the skills needed for Quadrant B: Application

Rigor/Relevance Framework™

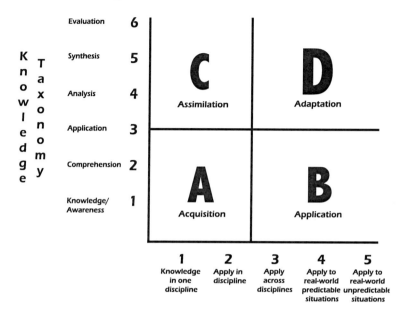

Application Model

and for Quadrant D: Adaptation. Measuring student success in Quadrants B or D requires the use of portfolios in authentic assessments.

Assessments: An Overview

Let's begin by reviewing some basic terms. Two of the most commonly interchanged terms are "evaluation" and "assessment." However, there is a distinction that should be made. *Assessment* means gathering information in order to make decisions about learning. *Evaluation* refers to judgments made as a result of information that has been gathered. Evaluations come in a variety of forms, including grades, adequate yearly progress (AYP) calculations for NCLB, and other reports. Assessments include various methods – both formal and informal – including written and oral tests as well as content- or performance-based measures. There are several forms of assessment, including:

Formative Assessment

Formative assessment involves gathering data on a periodic basis during instructional cycles. Formative assessments are usually administered and reviewed for a limited, internal school and classroom audience. The data collected through formative assessment provides an opportunity for student feedback by identifying strengths and weakness. Teachers also receive information that allows them to better tailor instruction to students' needs. Formative assessments are part of a comprehensive assessment plan; the results may or may not be used as part of students' grades.

Summative Assessments

Summative assessments are comprehensive in nature. They are given at the end of a unit, class, or course to ensure that students have met the applicable standards. Summative tests are often called "snapshots" because they provide a quick view of where the student is as of the test date. Examples include statewide tests, end-of-semester tests, mid-term exams, and final exams.

Criterion-Referenced Tests

Criterion-referenced tests (CRTs) measure performance against a specific objective. These tests are typically used to measure how well students have achieved a particular standard. CRTs typically determine individual performance or mastery of a standard, such as whether the student has learned the basics of algebra.

Norm-Referenced Tests

Norm-referenced tests (NRTs) are also called "standardized assessments" (even though they are not based on state standards). They provide a comparison of one student to another, producing a ranking of students from high-achieving to low-achieving.

Norm-referenced tests can provide diagnostic baselines at the beginning or the year, or provide insights into areas not covered by criterion-referenced testing. For example, an NRT might show one student's algebra knowledge compared to the class average.

Assessments FOR and OF Learning

Schools and districts use two types of student assessments: OF learning assessments and FOR learning assessments. OF learning assessment is summative, designed to show what students know at a particular point in the curriculum. FOR learning assessment is continuous, and data from this type of assessment is used to better inform instruction. These two categories are not absolutes, of course. Sometimes an assessment can be both an OF assessment and a FOR assessment. For example, teachers may combine periodic test scores with ongoing assessments of classroom progress to paint their own picture of a student's progress. But let's take a closer look at these tools.

OF Learning Assessment

Most public discussions about assessment consider data from OF learning assessments. The summative data this type of assessment provides a measure of a particular moment in time in terms of student learning. Before standardized testing became the norm, data from OF learning assessments was barely collected, unless it was needed for a transcript. However, OF learning data can yield a great deal of useful information. Educators are now beginning to use this assessment data to begin the process of student and teacher feedback, which may encourage program or curriculum evaluation.

For example, statewide testing under NCLB may indicate which subgroups or content need additional attention. A single summative assessment can bring questions and even more assessments. Instructional program or curriculum evaluation can be targeted to determine whether curriculum design supports all subgroups. Thus, end-of-course and end-of-year assessments provide feedback and ideas that can lead to improvements, including:

- reallocation of resources to help teachers and/or students
- prioritization of professional development to assist specific teachers
- realignment of the curriculum to increase student learning.

The assessment data can bring an initial analysis, then development of questions or suggestions to make changes or find additional data. The analysis can bring questions about students, instructions, programs, available money, and so forth. Moreover, OF learning assessment data can lead to discussions and decisions about needed changes.

OF learning assessments do have their limitations. For example, some maintain the data is unfair because it is a one-time snapshot. It may also seem inadequate for measuring student ability and knowledge. However, it can be helpful in beginning initial analysis, as well as in developing good follow-up questions and suggestions for allocating resources. The data also provides a good beginning or overview. Statewide assessments, a high profile version of an OF learning assessment, are based on common standards that address the question: "Are students able to use these standards at the appropriate grade level?"

When schools and districts only look at OF learning assessments, they focus on assessments at the end of a grading cycle, such as the end of the school year. Once the assessment is complete, the grade is final. Now the teacher and the student both go on to the next topic, or the next course, or maybe even the next year. OF assessments are often not considered useful for feedback to teachers, students or educational leaders as the majority of students simply move on to the next grade or class.

FOR Learning Assessment

Unlike OF learning assessment, FOR learning assessment occurs each day in the classroom. This type of formative assessment is generally considered a part of a continuing process under the teacher's control. FOR assessment produces a limited, yet important, set of data and is standards-based. This type of assessment:

- occurs as the student is moving toward full learning in terms of forming understandings and skills
- often is under the control of teacher groups, schools, or districts, as with some benchmark assessments
- enables teachers to assess student steps toward full understanding and application of the standards

More recently, research has focused on FOR learning assessment. Many educators now consider assessment an ongoing, essential, and methodical practice during the entire learning process. Continual classroom assessment can be designed to meet several objectives, such as

- finding out how the student is doing at specific stages (or benchmarks) during the learning process and at specific, periodic developmental points of the curriculum
- regularly and continually checking on progress (often using informal formative assessment) to ensure students are kept to a standard
- providing assessment results that can be used to start conversations between a teacher and a student with an end point or target in mind

Considered from this viewpoint, periodic, formative assessment is not an end but rather a beginning to the next stage in learning. FOR learning assessment positions the data as an essential component to the learning process when the:

- assessment is standards-based
- data is a critical part of the assessment
- assessment and data are critical elements of the learning process

In addition, there should be a continuing series of feedback cycles during the academic year within each classroom. Thus, at all times, teacher and student are joined in the learning/ assessment process as they work toward the ultimate goal: the OF learning assessment. Data from formative assessments drives decisions for the entire class, an individual student, and/or the teacher's instructional planning, including modifications.

OF Versus FOR Learning Assessment

Overall, both informal teacher formative assessment and the more formal benchmark formative assessment are part of the same continuum. Benchmark assessment is formative, but the formal process generally occurs at times prescribed by the school or the district. Informal assessment is directly controlled by the individual teacher.

It may sometimes be difficult to choose between formal and informal assessments, just as it may be challenging to choose between OF learning and FOR learning assessment. The two types of formative assessments may come together, depending upon such factors as a teacher's instructional plan or district policy. Plus, the assessment design may occur in several stages and may include both informal and formal measures.

A Systematic Approach:
Establishing Standards-Based Formative Assessments

There are a number of factors that allow formative assessment to occur systematically for all grades within a school. Those factors include leadership; curriculum development; types of assessments; shared data collection and analysis; student and parent understanding of the process; and support systems.

Leadership, as we know from Chapter 3, includes a school's principal and its teachers. Leadership must provide a budget, motivation, and time to enable changes in the structure for learning. Leaders need to focus on specific areas. Research shows leadership is most effective when it:

- creates a culture that supports change
- focuses on instruction instead of school structure
- respects students' personal relationships with peers and adults
- bases decisions on data

Curriculum development must be done jointly by the faculty. It should avoid simple textbook chapter lists, and instead firmly base decisions on standards, rigor, and relevance. A curriculum is successful when:

- The faculty agrees on benchmarking periods and uses them as critical steps in the learning process.
- The vertical curriculum for one school level, such as high school, is integrated as part of a system of learning so that transitions are smooth and planned.
- The horizontal curriculum is integrated; for example, mathematics and science curricula must be aligned so that students have the math knowledge to calculate required scientific formulas.

Assessments also need to be standards-based and benchmarked. Assessments and related items should be developed or agreed upon by the faculty. All rubrics for tests and projects should be shared with students. Where possible, formative assessments should build toward summative testing.

Data collection and analysis should also be shared among teachers. This allows teachers to share strategies for differentiated learning and assessment. They can also determine together whether an assessment actually measures a targeted benchmark.

It is also vital for students and parents to understand the process. Students are motivated when they are challenged to meet high expectations, when the relevance of the study area is transparent, and when academics can be seen in a real-life context. Assessment should not be a "gotcha" moment, but rather a step in the ongoing evaluation process. Parents also need as much information as students have if they are to be a true partner in the learning process. They need ongoing communication, not only in person from the teacher, but also through other methods, such as e-mail and online updates.

A number of supports are available for educators and students. These include software, computer-aided instruction, supplemental instruction, high expectations, and tutoring. These supports can be targeted toward:
- data collection and analysis
- differentiated learning
- tutoring
- motivation, interest, and curiosity
- assessments

Applying Assessments to Instruction

The value of assessment data for students, teachers, parents, schools, and districts goes beyond simply measuring school success and ensuring that students learn what they need to learn. Frequent and standards-based assessment is also essential to improving instruction.

Over the past 20 to 30 years, considerable attention has been paid to various instructional strategies, models, and reforms that educators should implement. Direct instruction has proven to be durable, with educators now being challenged to match "teacher talk" with learner needs, content goals, and standards-based outcomes. Considerable attention has been given to the ways educators can bring concepts such as cooperative learning, small-group learning, and brain-based instruction into their classrooms.

During this same time, however, little attention has been given to ways assessment might enhance approaches for increasing student performance. Most of the assessment focus has naturally gone to its use in state- or federally mandated high-stakes testing. And, for most teachers, prior to NCLB, their experiences with assessment were with weekly quizzes, end-of-chapter tests, or final exams. The emphasis on the high-stakes testing, including concern over the consequences of being classified as an underperforming school, however, has increased the perception that state tests are things that are "done *to* educators" rather than something that can be "done *for* educators."

Fortunately, more educators are shifting their focus. They realize the need to consider instruction and assessments together to help them focus on student achievement and student learning. There is a growing acknowledgement that assessment can provide feedback in the design and delivery of instruction.

Assessment data comes from various sources, and it is often presented in a variety of ways. Statewide data may be viewed as a whole or by subgroups, and it can be parsed into sub-content areas for a given subject area. The information can be presented as proficiency data, as with a percentage that indicates how many students achieved proficiency. It may also be in the form of scale scores, not true scores, but a technique that makes content scores easier to understand and compare by using a common scale from one year to the next.

Statewide assessments not only meet government requirements, they also provide basic data that drives decision making at the school and district levels. Data analysis begins the process of asking questions, allowing school and district personnel to work toward collecting additional targeted data.

While schools and districts have little control over statewide assessments, they can control the assessments they give during the year. They can design assessments to meet certain benchmarks or answer particular questions of local interest. "In-district" assessments are FOR learning measures and can vary in type. Such assessment data should support movement along the continuum from the beginning of the year to a target point, such as end-of-course or end-of-year assessment. Each assessment then becomes not an ending point but a beginning for the next phase of learning. And if students do not meet the standard, the class returns to instruction and learning.

Two specific types of assessment used within a district to help address the needs of all students are screening and diagnostic assessments. These assessments aim to identify specific problems that may interfere with a student's learning before instruction begins. Screening tests are not commonly used. Diagnostics are administered more frequently. In certain cases, diagnostic assessment is given after screening tests, and perhaps after some instruction has been modified based on screening results

A screening assessment is used to identify factors – such as readiness or a learning disability – that may have an impact on a student's ability to achieve in a content area. Screening assessments are generally developed by commercial companies. They are not standards-based but are norm-referenced.

Diagnostic assessments are specific and may be standards-based. A student may only need to be diagnosed deeply in one area, so the diagnostic helps an educator pinpoint the specific issue for a student. The diagnostic assessment differs from the formative assessment in that the diagnosis sets the course of action that must be taken, while the formative tests whether that course is working.

Diagnostic assessments are most often used for reading comprehension. They aim to identify students who are at risk in failing reading requirements. These assessments typically focus on five essential components of effective reading instruction:

- phonemic awareness, which is the understanding that individual sounds of spoken language work together to make words
- phonics, which describes the relationship between sounds of spoken words and the letters in written language that represent those sounds
- vocabulary, which is the ability to store information about the meaning and pronunciation of words
- fluency, which refers to the skill of reading text accurately and quickly, allowing readers to recognize and comprehend the words
- reading comprehension, which involves understanding, remembering, and communicating with others about what has been read

Feedback from a diagnostic assessment provides useful instructional guidance for the teacher and the student. Data from a diagnostic assessment should be explained to the student so that he or she can begin taking responsibility for learning. The student can practice certain skills or complete exercises at home. The teacher receives feedback about instruction for the individual student and for small-group settings. This feedback is used to modify the instruction so it better meets individual and group needs.

For all learners, teachers can also introduce standards-based benchmark assessments into their learning plans. Adding formative assessments means there is a need for more considered and planned testing during the year. Creating assessments for a unit or lesson follows development of the overall curriculum and should include these steps, in roughly this order:

- identify targeted standards and the points in the curriculum at which they should be assessed
- develop summative assessments
- develop formal, periodic formative, or benchmark,

assessments that are based on standards and are best devised by a group of teachers

- develop informal assessments, which are designed by each teacher

Once these measures are completed, the collection of classroom-level data and the interpretation of that data provide feedback to benefit individuals and groups of teachers, students, and parents. Classroom benchmark data is also useful to supervisors and administrators so they can monitor curricula to ensure timely standards-based learning. Schools and districts should try to choose more holistic or overview data, and review and interpret it in a framework of the school's mission or vision. At each level of review, however, good data and proper analysis are essential to providing meaningful information.

Keep It Real: Collecting and Communicating Assessment Data

On any given day, teachers – especially secondary school teachers – generally communicate to more people than any other school personnel. They communicate with administrators and colleagues, students and parents. To make this communication more demanding, an average elementary teacher has 30 students and a high school teacher may have up to 150.

With all the other communicating they do, teachers and school leaders must make sure they communicate the right information about assessments. For teachers, assessment means many things. It is what they do every day and every week – both formally and informally – throughout their careers. Most believe they have up-to-date information about how dozens of students are doing at any one time. However, sometimes the information they have is really more about impressions or expectations; it may not be based on true or sufficient data. Collecting real data helps ensure that the available information is useful and accurate, making their assessments and communications more accurate.

For school leaders, assessment also has many meanings. Leaders must communicate assessment information to many

149

audiences. They share information with community members, parents, school board members, teachers, and other school system leaders.

With so many listeners, leaders may need to vary the information they present. The level of detail, amount of information, and the presentation itself may differ with each audience. Each interest group may have its own unique viewpoint about the data's importance.

For teachers and school leaders alike, communication with all stakeholders can be challenging, but effective communication skills are essential when discussing data and assessment results with various parties. It is generally a good practice to provide a "big picture" view of the data during an early presentation and keeping detail to a minimum. This provides a good first step before moving on to more in-depth conversations with those audiences that want to know more.

Teachers and leaders must also understand their own communication styles to ensure effective interactions with individuals and groups. It is essential that they also understand the interests, needs, communication styles, and cultural differences of the various audiences they will address. This allows teachers and administrators to make the best decisions about how to present data.

Communication challenges are magnified when collecting and sharing data as required by NCLB. The law requires districts to report assessment data by both student subgroup and content. Before NCLB, most districts only reported general student scores to the public. Assessment data is now collected and reported for all NLCB subgroups, including race, socioeconomic status, and those with special educational needs and/or learning disabilities. In some situations, data for small subgroups may not be reported to the public, but the data is still collected.

Beyond NCLB, diagnostic data is often collected by individual teachers at the beginning of the school year to assess incoming students. As discussed earlier, diagnostic assessments are used to identify specific areas of weakness in order to better focus instruction for individual students and groups. Diagnostic assessments are often computer-based and are obtained through major publishing and education media companies. They often guide students to tutorials to support their weaker areas and give the teacher an opportunity to decide whether to intervene.

Assessment OF a school or program typically occurs through summative assessment and data collection. The most critical aspect of using data for OF assessment and evaluation of schools or programs is the data acquisition system. There are two types of summative data that schools and districts collect: statewide test results and in-school, end-of-year or end-of-term examination data.

The first step in reviewing assessment for school or program improvement is assessing current practices. Looking at the current data helps identify items that are absent or only partially represented, providing a starting point for creating a culture in which the system relies on the data for making decisions. In education, annual assessments, with their resulting summative data, offer the greatest opportunity to measure success. Summative data allows districts to decide whether the basic standards are being met.

Good schools are also interested in seeing how students are doing along the way. To do so, they must take a deeper look at data from the assessments OF the programs. The data shows where student performance falls in relationship to their goals and benchmarks. They look for information that identifies areas for additional exploration as they continue working to improve their academic programs.

The use of only summative data is not sufficient, however; yet, mid-course adjustments should not be based on intuition. In order to know what corrections should be made, and to evaluate those currently in process, it is essential to gather information more than once a year and in greater detail than is provided by large-scale assessment projects, such as statewide tests. This is where formative data – FOR learning data – is required.

There are multiple times when formative assessments FOR learning can be obtained during a marking period, term, or school year. These opportunities should be made explicit to students and parents. Multiple formative points, including benchmarks, in the curriculum should be clearly marked, and these should explicitly and directly relate to standards. A calendar can be developed with points for each formative assessment. Districts that involve teachers in developing benchmarking tests find that including teachers facilitates buy-in of the process.

In addition, teachers regularly collect data for assessments through tests, quizzes, projects or portfolios. All this assessment data should be linked to both standards and student thinking levels, particularly benchmark. Teachers should have access to online or computer-based grade books to ease the process of calculating this data, as well as to make it easier to submit information to a central, electronic storage area. Supervisors should provide teachers with student scores from previous years, which can help teachers with instructional planning for incoming classes.

Overall, data collection is an ongoing system that should take place at several stages of the learning process. The collection should be in a form that is helpful to the user, and data should always be collected with that goal in mind. While some data cannot be shared with the general public – such as when a subgroup is too small for results to be publicly reported – it should be shared with educational professionals, as appropriate.

Summative data from both content and sub-content areas provides a critical starting point and should be shared among teachers of the same content area. The information also may be shared with teachers of other content areas, as appropriate, so teachers can work together to provide student support across the curriculum.

If schools want to move beyond assessment OF programs to assessment FOR programs, they must be prepared to look more deeply at the data and what it means. They must be prepared to gather formative as well as summative data so that program evaluation is ongoing and can be modified mid-course, if needed.

The most effective way of making school improvements is by engaging in dialogue about improvement so effective action plans can be developed. School leaders must ensure that they communicate effectively with all stakeholders to ensure a mutually beneficial outcome for all concerned.

152

CHAPTER EIGHT

Making the Case
for Success:

Refining the Process on an
Ongoing Basis

The reforming of American schools and the improvement of student achievement is a journey that never ends. I learned early on as a classroom teacher and as a coach that what works one year needs to be refined and retooled the next year. The same can be said for overall school reform.

Each set of students brings a different set of skills, knowledge, and challenges. Each passing year brings new innovations in creativity that we need to consider. Each year show us practices that worked in the past, but that are now no longer successful. Technology continues to evolve at a rapid pace, affecting everything it touches. For these reasons and others, school reform needs to be an ongoing process – one that is never considered complete – and, as educators, we ourselves need to be lifelong learners.

At the International Center, we continuously evaluate the nation's most successful schools, and each year, we select and showcase these schools in a wide variety of settings. Case studies document the practices of the nation's most successful schools. The nation's highest performing schools are showcased at our annual Model Schools Conference. We encourage schools to participate in an annual national symposium, where we ask individual school's leadership teams to carefully reexamine their practices and compare them to those at the nation's most successful schools. This leads to the continuous tweaking or refining that is the hallmark of the school reform process.

Here we present seven inspiring profiles of schools around the country that have embraced school improvement as a challenging but ongoing process, a process that demands careful, focused scrutiny that is guided by the components we have talked about throughout this book. The International Center has worked closely with all of them over the years.

A.B. Combs Leadership Magnet Elementary School
Raleigh, North Carolina

Overview

The A. B. Combs Leadership Magnet Elementary School program is grounded in the belief that building cooperative relationships and nurturing responsibility, kindness, and good judgment are the basis for creating a successful community of learners. By developing the whole child –socially, emotionally, academically, and ethically – the program fosters a climate of principle-centered and personal leadership. It is the school's culture of continuous improvement and performance excellence, differentiated instruction, curriculum integration, real-world problem solving, academic rigor, and embracing diversity that makes it the district's leading school of choice. What was once thought impossible – a learning-centered paradigm that focuses on leadership development in young children – is now being replicated at schools across the country.

The Wake County Public School System is the second largest in North Carolina. Its 147 schools had a total enrollment of 128,000 students for the 2006–07 school year. Combs Elementary School, an urban school in the capital city of Raleigh, is tucked into a diverse neighborhood between North Carolina State University and Research Triangle Park. If you were to walk into Combs, you would be awash in a sea of diversity, with 805

154

students from 64 countries speaking 28 different languages. Combs is one of the few public schools offering instruction for the deaf and hard of hearing. With the largest elementary international population in the district, Combs also provides instruction for English language learners (ELLs). Diversity of students in the district's schools is maintained through the use of socioeconomic and academic achievement indicators. The district objectives are for all schools to be below 40 percent free- or reduced-lunch status and for no school to have more than 25 percent of its students performing below grade level. These objectives are intended to help all students meet the district's "Goal 2008," which states that "98 percent of students in grades 3 through 12 are at or above grade level by 2008, and all student groups will demonstrate high growth."

Program Components

A decade ago, Combs was faced with the mandate to reinvent itself, or to cease and desist. Dwindling enrollment and mediocre test scores threatened the school's magnet status. Today, Combs is considered a national leader in the creation of a new learning-centered paradigm that focuses on leadership development in young children. The school has developed an innovative model that integrates Dr. Stephen Covey's philosophy of leadership development and the Baldrige National Quality Program's Criteria for Performance Excellence. *The Seven Habits of Highly Effective People* is the driving force behind the day-to-day activities of students and staff.

Combs' curriculum serves the broad goals for student learning based on national standards, research, and best practices. The school has a goal-setting, risk-taking staff committed to performance excellence, students' active learning, and the development of real-world problem-solving skills. Teachers have been trained in applying the Baldrige criteria to their own and their students' performance goals. These criteria are built on a set of interrelated core values and concepts: learning-centered education, management by fact, agility, focusing on the future and managing for innovation, systems perspective, and a focus on results and creating value.

155

As a result of infusing the Baldrige practices and using quality tools, data collection and analysis, problem-based learning, and rubric development in the classroom, students are empowered as decision makers and leaders of their own learning. At Combs, assessment drives instruction. Formative assessment is used to measure learning early in the learning process, allowing teachers to fine-tune their instructional strategies to respond most effectively to their students' individual needs. Quarterly benchmark assessments allow individual and grade level analysis.

The school constantly asks itself, "How can we help our students make wise choices, both personally and academically?" At Combs, these choices are reflected in students taking responsibility for their actions and doing their best in all areas of their lives.

Combs strives to align classroom instruction with student achievement. Many different assessment techniques are used to reflect student progress, including:

- Eliminating random acts of improvement: To ensure that everything is aligned with the vision and mission, leaders examine each initiative to validate its place in student achievement. Staff and students have developed criteria for excellence, then designed and adopted rubrics that resulted in significant increases in the caliber and quality of students' project-based work.

- Data notebooks and student-led conferences: At the beginning of each nine-week period, children, in collaboration with their parents and teacher, set their own personal and academic goals. Progress toward these goals is charted daily in their data notebooks, which serve as the basis for quarterly student-led parent-teacher conferences.

- Victory folders and self-assessment: Each week, children are given the opportunity to reflect about their work and select samples of their finest efforts to be placed in their Victory Folders, creating a portfolio of student work that charts progress over the course of the year.

156

- Achievement as measured by standardized tests: According to the state standards, schools with more than 90 percent of end-of-grade test scores at or above grade level are designated as "Schools of Excellence" by the state's board of education. Combs has earned this distinction for several years. The school attributes the sustained increase in test scores to the implementation of time-sensitive procedures that review student assessment results, which allows teachers to make "just-in-time" adjustments in curriculum and instruction.

The Combs community is the embodiment of the African proverb: "It takes a village to raise a child." A dynamic PTA and members of the community organize and host annual events, such as a fall festival, Inaugural Ball, science fair, art show, International Festival, and book fair. They have forged partnerships with area universities that afford students and staff the unprecedented opportunity to learn with the area's leading scientists and educators. Students understand that true leaders give back to their communities. Each grade level team of students adopts a community service project, such as collecting toys for needy children, conducting a winter coat drive, or raising funds for the Duke University Cancer Ward. Students also give back through schoolwide efforts, such as collecting canned goods for the North Carolina Food Bank.

Combs listens to its stakeholders through quarterly "coffee talks" with parents and community members and monthly "children's chats." Twice each year, each classroom teacher, administrator, and specialist sends surveys home to collect feedback from parents. In addition, a Leadership Advisory Council, made up of parents and community leaders, provides feedback for the school's leadership initiatives.

Evidence of the uniqueness, strength, and success of the Combs Leadership Magnet Elementary School model is reflected in the sustained rise of the end-of-grade test scores. Combs created and implemented a new learning-centered, leadership-focused paradigm in the throws of burgeoning enrollment (a 25 percent increase) and equally daunting increases in the number of ELL, free-and-reduced lunch, and special-needs students. In just five years, the percentage of students performing at or above grade level rose from 85 percent in 1999 to 98 percent in 2003. What once seemed like an impossible dream is now an inspiring model.

Albion Central School District
Albion, New York

Overview

The spring of 1998 brought a new challenge to Albion Central School (ACS). Like many school districts across the nation, Albion was facing increased numbers of teacher retirements, new positions created to reduce class size, and a shortage of qualified professionals to fill these vacancies. Getting, training, and keeping new teachers became a challenge. And although ACS's percentage of teacher attrition was not as gloomy as the national average, it was time to act.

In the late 1990s, Albion developed Professionals Helping Professionals, a multiyear program designed to provide support for Albion's new teachers by easing the transition from preparation to practice and improving instructional skills to maximize student achievement. New teachers now attend a preservice summer institute that provides them with a solid understanding of district's initiatives, expectations, and standards applicable to ACS, as outlined by the education board.

In the first year of the program, new teachers are assigned a master-level "buddy teacher." They are given quarterly release time for planning. Additionally, the program's first year features opportunities for classroom/peer visitations and reflections; monthly mini-workshops about issues and concerns pertinent to novice professionals; team-teaching; social activities; and comprehensive staff development. A district mentor/coordinator provides support in the classroom, plans and reflects with new teachers and buddy-teachers, and is always available for emotional support and encouragement. In the second and third year, time is scheduled bimonthly for sharing concerns and instructional strategies; in-house workshops are provided to expand and improve best practices; and professional growth and development is stressed. Individual teacher growth plans are developed for teachers who need additional support at the end of each of the first two years.

Professionals Helping Professionals is meeting the challenge at ACS. Performance levels in the classrooms of new teachers in the program – and graduates of the program – are well above district's expectations, as evidenced by performance evaluations. ACS's novice teachers are significantly responsible for the school's academic successes. In addition, teacher attrition has dwindled to less than 4 percent.

Program Components

When combined, the individual components of the Professionals Helping Professionals program add up to high teacher retention and academic success for students:

Preservice Summer Institute: Teachers attend a seven-day preservice institute on site, which includes a community tour and luncheon along with initial training in Charlotte Danielson's *Enhancing Professional Practice: A Framework for Teaching.* Additional topics include community and parent involvement, planning and preparation, classroom management, character education, rigor and relevance, service learning, classroom and behavior management, learner engagement, and technology.

Three-Year Professional Development Plan: New teachers complete a comprehensive, multiyear professional development program designed to strengthen instructional methodologies, enhance professional practice, and increase student achievement.

Mentoring: Novice educators are assigned a master-level buddy teacher who has been trained as a teacher-mentor and who provides guidance, support, and feedback, as defined by program expectations. The "mentor-mentee" team meets weekly to complete peer observations, plan for and arrange release days, team-teach, develop and assess lessons, share strategies and best practices, reflect on professional practice, and celebrate successes.

Individual Performance Growth Plans: Beginning in the second year of the program, performance evaluations of teachers in the program are closely monitored for patterns in performance levels. Using Albion's Annual Professional Growth Plan, which was developed to reflect the assessment criteria in Danielson's *Framework,* teachers who fail to meet the district's performance expectations are further supported with an individual performance growth plan. These plans target the specific components of practice a new teacher is struggling with and provide individualized blueprints for improvement. Interventions, support personnel, time frames, and performance benchmarks are clearly defined. Teachers needing extra time to meet "proficient" performance levels are most often given another year in the program.

ACS believes that novice teachers have the potential to be successful as educators within its framework. If a probationary teacher is still struggling by the end of the third year, he or she engages in dialogue with district and building level administration to ascertain if the lack of performance is related to skill deficiencies or a philosophical mismatch. Participation in the induction program will clearly affect teacher effectiveness; however, it is unrealistic to think a school district has the power to change a personal belief system.

Program Assessment: Each year, all stakeholders involved in the induction program – administrators, the mentor coordinator, new teachers, and buddy teachers – complete a comprehensive program evaluation. Goals and objectives, criteria, components, and performance results are scrutinized to determine whether programmatic changes are needed.

Professionals Helping Professionals is working well for Albion. Its impact is statistically significant, not only in attracting and retaining highly qualified young professionals, but also in dramatically improving the teaching quality of newly hired educators. Student achievement across the district is up, teacher attrition and migration is down, and novice teachers are reaching proficient and distinguished performance levels faster and with fewer challenges than ever before.

Of 86 new teachers hired over a five-year period, 82 were still teaching at ACS. One hundred percent of these new teachers reached or surpassed expected performance levels in all elements of planning and preparation, classroom environment, and instruction. Student achievement is greater in the classrooms of teachers currently in the program, or graduates of the program, as compared with that of other teachers. Graduation rates at ACS – defined as students graduating with their cohort – have markedly increased. Over the past five years, the percentage of seniors graduating with a Regents diploma has steadily increased, as well.

Albion's commitment to its new educators is comprehensive and systematic. Professionals Helping Professionals provides the resources necessary to nurture, develop, and maintain its highly skilled novice teachers. As a result, Albion's new professionals feel valued, supported, and confident in their abilities to meet the demands of teaching and the expectations outlined by the district. The bottom line: Trained teachers are effective teachers. Districts that provide structured, sustained training for their teachers achieve what every school district seeks to achieve: improved student learning.

Brockton High School
Brockton, Massachusetts

Overview

Brockton High School is a comprehensive grade 9-12 high school located in an urban center 30 miles south of Boston. The school's 4,350 students represent a range in diversity and socioeconomic levels. The education program follows a six-day block schedule that offers core and elective courses in academic, vocational, fine arts, and performing arts programs. High expectations and high standards help motivate students enrolled in each of four levels: advanced placement, advanced, college preparatory, and academic preparatory.

The school began a restructuring process in 1995 to increase student achievement and provide a more personalized educational experience for all students. A literacy initiative to improve student skills by having all teachers assume responsibility for literacy instruction within their classes has improved student performance to the point that the school was recognized as a Commonwealth Compass School by the state. As part of the initiative to establish smaller learning communities, students are now assigned to one of four houses to ensure closer working relationships with teachers and to enable teachers to gain greater knowledge of student interests and career aspirations. Recent initiatives, including a freshman academy and academic success programs, are now underway to increase the rigor and relevance of the curriculum and to support 9th grade students in the difficult transition year to high school.

The school has a long history and tradition of success in sports and performing arts. Extracurricular activities are numerous, and more than 3,500 students participated in one or more of these activities during the past year. The school makes consistent use of data to evaluate programs and to pinpoint areas in need of new or revised programming. Administrators operate in a collaborative and supportive fashion, involving faculty in decision making and ownership of key school initiatives.

The school culture is student-focused and positive, which has resulted in success in improving students' academic performance while maintaining the tradition of achievement in performing arts, theater, and athletics. The school is dedicated to continuous improvement with a diverse population and an experienced faculty, many of whom grew up in the city where they now teach.

Program Components

A cornerstone of the school's successful improvement efforts is the creation of positive relationships among administrators, faculty, and students. These relationships are built on trust, vision, and consistency. The Brockton Public Schools system maintains a clear vision of the type of educational institution it wishes to be and how it will provide a high-quality education that motivates and engages all students. Over the past five years, the school district has publicly and consistently maintained the challenge for all its employees that its schools will:

- provide literacy in reading, writing, speaking, and reasoning
- use best practices for effective instruction
- have access to technology in support of teaching and learning
- provide ongoing evaluation and revision of courses and programs
- address standards set by state and national agencies
- establish high academic standards using a variety of assessment instruments
- foster effective communication among staff, students, parents, families, and the community
- continue efforts to increase the personalization of education for all students
- examine the senior year
- seek ways to improve community outreach
- improve in-house suspension

The policies, programs, and activities represent tangible steps to achieve the goals and mission promulgated in the school improvement plan. The administration and faculty annually review the perceived strengths of the school and identify new initiatives to address areas of need. A Restructuring Committee is a vehicle to highlight and review issues related to the school's efforts to achieve its overarching goals: to increase student achievement levels and to personalize education for all students. The 27-member committee represents academic areas, resource staff, and administration. Challenging issues currently receiving focus are:

- transitioning from junior high to high school
- scheduling
- raising academic expectations for all students
- improving school and classroom culture
- personalization

- examining the senior year
- advancing technology

The school has identified these factors as the most significant elements of its success:

- School leadership: School leaders foster collaborative decision making among faculty and support a more personalized educational experience through smaller learning communities. The superintendent and principal have used district and building resources to develop a rigorous curriculum and to make instruction relevant. Administrative leadership practices the concept of "top-down support for bottom-up leadership." Teachers express a degree of ownership in decision making and have a high feeling of professionalism.
- Literacy initiative: This effort focuses instruction on vocabulary, comprehension, and speaking as well as on writing open-response essays and research papers. The use of best practices in staff development and displays of scoring rubrics and literacy charts in each classroom give faculty a common purpose and language in the pursuit of schoolwide goals.
- Restructuring Committee: This committee has had a significant impact on the culture of achievement and student performance levels. The goals of the committee are to increase student achievement and to provide a personalized educational experience.
- Safety nets: The school has safety nets to support students with academic needs, students with disabilities, and English language learners, including after-school tutoring, an access center, directed academic programs, freshman summer academies, inclusion programs, and adult advisement programs. Support programs at the school include school adjustment counselors, a school nursery, wellness centers, and programs for nutrition, stress reduction, and peer mediation.
- Instructional support: The use of special support personnel is a valuable adjunct to content teachers. The

instructional resource specialist, teacher mentors, and informational resource centers provide instructional assistance to teachers. Office units provide face-to-face, informal, daily assistance to teachers for sharing and discussions.

- Passion for teaching: Teachers enjoy working with young people and treat students as adults. Teachers capitalize on the advantages of humor in the classroom and demonstrate a respect for other teachers, students, and community members. They seek to instill a work ethic in course offerings and internships to help students succeed.
- Small group instruction: Instruction frequently occurs in small work groups that emphasize vocabulary, information processing, and writing and note-taking to ensure participation. The faculty maintains a student focus with motivating questions, discussions of relevancy, frequent checks of learning, and individual assistance.
- Civility: Students have a sense of civility, purpose, and discipline necessary to achieve. Student rules of conduct are provided in a handbook and are supported by teachers and housemasters.
- Support for families: The faculty and administration pursue ethnic clubs, parent involvement from ethnic groups, and instructional programs that support English language learners.
- Use of data: Staff maintains a "target and response" approach to the use of data. Data is shared with the community to demonstrate student performance levels and areas needing improvement.
- Search for excellence: The school strives for excellence in curriculum and extracurricular areas. Time, effort, and resources are devoted to support student interests and abilities in sports, arts, music, drama, JROTC, and academic competitions.

English Estates Elementary School
Fern Park, Florida

Overview

English Estates Elementary School is at the beginning of a journey from a promising school to a proven school. In recent years, the school implemented Leadership is Elementary as the basis of its continuous improvement efforts. Like most schools, English Estates had many superb strategies and programs in place and had some success with student achievement. As a school with increasing diversity, increasing levels of poverty, high mobility, and a growing population of non-English-speaking students, leaders realized they needed to make changes to address the growing achievement gap and to meet high expectations. They needed to analyze the data, understand the root causes of issues, improve alignment, make their plan cohesive, and ensure that the entire staff was committed to a common vision and mission. Now, as the school continues to implement the plan, it faces the challenges of remaining true to its vision and building and sustaining a school culture that supports rigor, relevance, and relationships.

Seminole County Public Schools, located in suburban Orlando, serves 68,000 students. Built more than 40 years ago to serve a suburban community, English Estates Elementary School is now an urban fringe school serving a diverse student population. For many years, the school enjoyed active parent involvement and high student achievement. Over the past two decades, however, the area has taken on the characteristics of a more urban community, serving students from more than 20 apartment and condominium complexes. It recently experienced an unusual drop in enrollment as families were displaced by rising rent costs, rising home and insurance costs, hurricane fears, and a large number of condominium conversions.

Program Components

In April 2004, several factors influenced a change in school culture at English Estates. A new principal was appointed, completion of a new building added additional student enrollment, and the school board approved additional funds to develop a Program of Emphasis at the school. During the 2004-2005 school year, a committee of teachers and parents was established to research and investigate various options. Learning from other models has helped English Estates develop better quality initiatives. The school followed the 10 Key Components Fundamental to School Improvement as identified by the Successful Practices Network. Using the dimensions of the Learning Criteria to Support 21st Century Learners – core academic learning, stretch learning, learner engagement, and personal skill development – has also helped staff focus on the most important things. During the 2005-06 school year, the plan was implemented and English Estates soon showed some exciting gains in student achievement.

Florida's *Sunshine State Standards* are the framework for the curriculum in the core areas. Unfortunately, there are so many standards that it is hard to focus on the most important. One of the critical things English Estates has done is narrow the standards down to the most important in terms of state assessments. Frequent progress monitoring has given teachers data to guide instruction. The entire school has learned more about analyzing data and using data through regular team meetings and professional development. Teachers maintain a class data notebook with the results of progress monitoring in reading, writing, and mathematics. This process has illuminated several common problems that the school is now tackling: lack of common data sources for grades K-5; too much data that is not useful; repetitive paperwork; lack of knowledge about how to use data to guide instruction; and the difficulty in finding effective interventions.

One of the most successful strategies the school has adopted is the use of student data notebooks. Students in grades K-5 share responsibility for their own individual progress monitoring. As a part of the student data notebooks, each student sets goals and develops action plans to achieve them for each grading period. Evaluation and progress monitoring are a part of the plan. While time-consuming initially, it has been successful in helping students see their progress and accept responsibility for their learning.

Student-led conferences have empowered students to take a more active role in their education. They have also led to more parental involvement. Classes that have fully implemented student-led conferences report 100 percent parent participation, doubling the average of about 50 percent participation. Student recognition is also a part of learner engagement. Students can receive recognition as a Leader of the Week, a Writer of the Week, or a variety of other awards.

Relationships and personal skill development have also been keys to the school's progress. Having staff spending a week together before the start of the school year enhanced the collective vision of what English Estates Elementary should be and do as a school. Opportunities are provided for parents to learn, as well as to share opinions and give feedback. Teachers are involved in the decision-making process at English Estates and are encouraged to take the initiative in improving the school's practices.

Team leaders, a collaborative improvement team, a Successful Practices Network study group, a school advisory council, a literacy support team, and a behavioral support team – in addition to many other teams and committees – are integral parts of the school, leading to improved practices and procedures for the benefit of all. Other successful activities include:

- a standardized dress code
- student plan books
- peer mediation
- a behavior intervention team
- a teacher support team
- a staff mentoring program
- a THREAD team: Together Happily Reinforcing Educationally Appropriate Discipline

English Estates also strives to be a community school. Parents, business partners, and community organizations play critical roles in the school's success:

- D÷v÷dend Volunteers is the broad moniker for the school's volunteer programs, which include Math

Superstars, Super Scientists, Digalo en Espanol, Reading Acceleration Program (RAP), and many other volunteer options.

- All-Pro Dads involves dads or other male role models who join their children for breakfast and participate in fun activities.
- Rotary Club of Casselberry hosts a variety of activities to benefit the school, including the annual Take a Kid Fishin' Day, which is used as an incentive for attendance, good behavior, and reading.
- Casselberry Chamber of Commerce helped English Estates host an event during American Education Week to showcase Leadership Is Elementary. Business leaders and community members were awed by the poise, knowledge, and graciousness of the school's students.
- Leadership Partnership enables individuals and businesses to adopt a classroom. Among other activities, classroom sponsors help enhance classroom libraries and develop a personal relationship with the class.

In a short time, English Estates has already seen success. Students have taken charge of their own learning, as evidenced in their understanding and use of goal setting, charting their own learning in student data notebooks, and student-led conferences that have increased parent attendance at parent-teacher events. The processes now underway are making an impact on student achievement.

Fort Worth Independent School District
Fort Worth, Texas

Overview

The Fort Worth Independent School District (FWISD) serves about 80,200 students in grades pre-K -12. The district's 144 school campuses include 80 elementary schools, 24 middle schools, 13 high schools, and 27 alternative schools. The fourth largest school district in Texas, Fort Worth ISD has taken strong, positive steps toward achieving the goal of becoming the best urban school district in the nation.

The district has instituted *Vision 2010*, a series of initiatives to redesign, transform, and revitalize FWISD schools, especially the ambitious commitment to reforming the district's 13 comprehensive high schools. Rather than create single islands of excellence, Fort Worth has embraced the challenge of systemic reform of its secondary schools in order to create and sustain a lasting impact in how schooling is approached in middle and high school.

Under the new strategic plan, the bar has been raised, with defined expectations that all FWISD students will:

- be actively engaged as learners in a rigorous curriculum
- attend schools that are caring and supportive learning communities
- be known by teachers in a personalized environment that meets individual needs
- benefit from highly competent teachers who are held accountable to rigorous standards
- graduate well prepared for postsecondary education and gainful employment and to be contributing citizens to Fort Worth and the nation.

FWISD has a student ethnicity breakdown of 27.1 percent African-American, 55.1 percent Hispanic, 15.9 percent Anglo, 1.7 percent Asian/Pacific Islander, and 0.2 percent Native American. Additionally, 25.4 percent of the district's enrollment is Limited English Proficient, 70.6 percent economically disadvantaged, and 9.0 percent requiring special education services.

In 2006, FWISD graduated 3,587 students, of which 2,960 graduated on the state's Recommended High School Program or the Distinguished Achievement Program. Twenty-two National Merit semifinalists came from the district's high schools. In 2005-2006, 1,510 students districtwide took the SAT with an average score of 936. FWISD's most recently recorded dropout rate was 1.2 percent. On the state accountability exam – the Texas Assessment of Knowledge and Skills, or TAKS – 81 percent of 9th graders met the standard in reading and 43 percent met the standard in mathematics. At the 10th grade level, 79 percent met the standard in English/language arts, 52 percent met the standard in mathematics, 48 percent met the standard in science, and 77 percent met the standard in social studies. The trend of achievement continues into 11th grade, in which 83 percent of students met the standard in English/language arts, 69 percent met the standard in mathematics, 65 percent met the standard in science, and 91 percent met that standard in social studies.

Program Components

In 2005, the Secondary School Leadership Department was given the task of developing a theory of action for Fort Worth ISD detailing how to bring about change in the way schooling is done at the baker's dozen of comprehensive high schools within the district. Later that year, *The Theory of Action for World-Class Schools,* known more commonly by its shorthanded *Theory of Action*, was developed to provide a framework to accomplish clearly defined goals for students as well as to lay the groundwork for further FWISD reforms at all levels.

The *Theory of Action* has served as the basis for a strategic plan that honors and builds upon the unique character, qualities, and resources of Fort Worth. While designs may differ from campus to campus, there are three over-arching principles that guide and assess the school reform implementation plan for all schools: 1) academic rigor in a thinking curriculum, 2) personalization leading to an improved culture and climate, and 3) effective, accountable leadership.

The *Theory of Action*'s implementation involved a number of steps, which has resulted in a wide range of programs and initiatives to support students and teachers:

- A sustained professional development program, created with the assistance of the International Center for Leadership in Education, is in place.
- Each high school developed and now uses a pyramid of academic interventions to assist teachers in determining specific actions to take as students began to fail. The guiding principle in this effort is "to catch kids before they fail."

- The district created 9th grade academies on the campuses of all 13 high schools. Most academies are separated from the rest of the students in a section of the building, and many campuses have a separate lunch for 9th grade students.
- 9th grade students are now assigned to teams of teachers in the core academic areas.
- Team meetings are held daily with the express purpose of getting to know students better, to create a more caring learning environment, and to intervene sooner if students begin to struggle academically. An assistant principal and counselor are assigned to the teams to monitor for effectiveness. Intervention specialists and stay-in-school coordinators are also involved. Conferences with students and their parents are conducted during the team meeting time.
- Academic Learning Plans (ALPs) were developed and introduced to help the district's high schools assist students in developing plans for life after high school. Students now track their accumulation of graduation credits; determine courses they wish to take in the future; receive assistance with college admission essays, letters of recommendation, and samples of exemplary work; and increase their awareness of college and career options and opportunities.
- During the summer, transition camps are held at all of the district's high schools and middle schools for students moving from grade 5 to grade 6 as well as from grade 8 to grade 9. The program focuses on three components: academics transition, with a focus on math and science, social transition, and school culture. About 3,500 students typically participate in the camps.
- Project Prevail was introduced and is now a comprehensive effort to increase the number of students graduating from Fort Worth high schools fully prepared for postsecondary education or gainful employment.
- The district has instituted an effort-based learning model through the Institute for Learning. The model supports the

belief that through directed, sustained, and appropriate effort, all students are capable of rigorous thinking and can achieve a uniformly high academic standard.

- A content coaching model is in place at all high schools and middle schools. The goal of the model is to improve the quality of teaching and learning taking place in secondary school classrooms through the use of master teachers known as Lead Content Teachers.

Fort Worth's achievements continue to grow as the program matures. System staff has learned a number of lessons, including:

- Start early: Trying to create systemic change takes time. It is very important to determine a rollout date and to plan backwards from there. Give yourself plenty of leeway as time – second only to money – is the greatest constraint you will face.
- Never assume initial training is adequate: Sustained professional development is critical.
- Revisit the mission and vision for change: This is crucial for all activities.
- Fidelity to implementation is crucial: Being sensitive to the perspectives of others as well as the ability to compromise is important; however, it is essential to stay focused on the mission and vision for change.
- People must own the change: Until the need for change is made morally compelling and internalized, action will not take place. People must feel that the success or failure of the change initiative rests in the actions – or inaction – they take.
- You must take something off the plate of those enacting the change: Piling on more by creating a bigger plate does not create a recipe for success.
- Provide the highest quality, sustained professional development for lasting change.

173

Kennesaw Mountain High School
Kennesaw, Georgia

Overview

Opened in 2002, Kennesaw Mountain High School serves the northwest area of Cobb County, Georgia, which is home to the second largest school system in the state and the 30th largest in the country. Kennesaw Mountain is a growing suburban school supported by a growing community. In 2006-2007, the district's 3,100 students were served by 225 certified staff members. The student population comprised 71 percent Caucasian, 15 percent African-American, 7 percent Hispanic, 4 percent Asian, and 3 percent students of other ethnic backgrounds. Student subgroups included students with disabilities (9.8 percent of the student population), gifted students (18.3 percent), English language learners (1.3 percent) and students receiving free- or reduced-lunch benefits (14 percent). The dropout rate was 3 percent.

Students at Kennesaw Mountain choose from a variety of class offerings consistent with other Cobb County high schools. Numerous electives and academic courses, including honors, inclusion, and advanced placement (AP) classes, are offered to students who are obtaining college preparatory and technology/career diplomas. The school offers a total of 118 core courses, including 25 AP courses and 174 elective courses in 13 curricular areas. About 525 students take AP exams. The average class size is 26 students.

Kennesaw Mountain operates on a four-period block schedule and organizes the communities within the school into additional academies, or houses, to provide more personalized educational opportunities. The school has a strong commitment to ensure that no student is allowed to fall through the cracks. The commitment to put students first is so strong, in fact, that students who drop out of school are kept on the rolls and contacted periodically by the staff to let them know that the school is still open to them.

The school recognizes the challenges that it will face during the next few years, especially in terms of growth and diversity. Staff members realize that they must continually evaluate their programs to ensure that they are meeting the needs of all of their students. Students are held to high expectations and are supported

174

in numerous ways. It is clear throughout the building that students are valued. This culture of respect is due in large part to highly visible and successful service learning and character education programs. The staff has a passion for meeting the needs of students and support from the administration to do so.

The overriding characteristic of the school is leadership. Multiple levels of leadership exist within the school. The principal created an environment that demands high standards for all students. The commitment to those standards is carried out by the assistant principals, instructional leaders, classroom teachers, students, parents, and community members. As one student remarked: "It's cool to be smart."

The school makes an extraordinary commitment to, and has great success in, its special education program. Students with disabilities are held to the same high standards as all students and are supported to achieve them. Numerous resource courses are available and are either team-taught in mainstream classrooms or delivered in self-contained classes. These classes include most of the core courses in the major academic disciplines that are offered to all students. In addition, resource course options include study and social skills, work-study, and reading enrichment.

Program Components

During Kennesaw Mountain's short history, success has been achieved in both academic and extracurricular programs. Student scores on the Georgia High School Graduation Test have shown improvement in most areas during the past four years, and school surpasses the district and state averages in all academic areas. Notable are the performance in science and social studies. In science, 90 percent of Kennesaw students met or exceeded state standards compared to 83 percent in the district and 76 percent in the state. In social studies, 96 percent of Kennesaw students met or exceeded standards compared to the 93 percent of district and 89 percent of state students who did so.

The school's commitment to a rigorous and relevant curriculum for all students is reflected in the course offerings and organizational structures. Through vertical teaming and other initiatives, faculty members work with feeder schools to identify students with the potential to be successful in honors and AP courses. These students, and their parents, are invited to presentations before they enter high school. Once they enter the school, they are assisted academically as they prepare for upper level courses. With 25 AP courses along with a plethora of honors and magnet program classes, Kennesaw Mountain has a challenging curriculum and encourages all students to engage in it. Currently, 41 percent of the student body is enrolled in honors and/or AP courses.

One unique opportunity is the Mountain Top Café, which is run by students with disabilities. Each day participating students oversee preparation and sales of different coffee beverages to students and staff. These students are developing important life skills – teamwork, problem solving, individual accountability – that will prepare them for the future. The café's staff members are considered employees, and it is their responsibility to oversee the operation of the business including inventory, purchasing, paying rent, and distributing salaries. The tremendous success of this student-run business provides these students, who are not in a traditional academic environment, with an opportunity for recognition of the daily achievements they make.

A commitment to student achievement is paramount at Kennesaw Mountain. Recognizing that not all students enter high school with the same skills, the faculty has adopted a school performance goal that includes reducing gaps in student achievement by engaging all students in a rigorous and relevant curriculum. In a culture that encourages teachers to question paradigms and "think outside the box," teachers feel free to be innovative as they make learning challenging for their students.

School leaders identify the following factors as the most significant in the school's achievements.
- Leadership is key to the school's success.
- Staff members are always seeking ways to personalize education for students through such efforts as the academy and magnet programs.
- Extracurricular and interscholastic activities are viewed as ways to personalize the high school experience and to get to know the students.

- Two staff members are deployed full time to critical areas of need; one administrator focuses on student leadership and high expectations for all students while the other focuses on teaching and learning.
- Service learning and character education are embedded in everything that happens in the school; it is evident in the way the students treat each other and in the relationships between the adults and the students.
- Conversation centers on learning and student needs. Decisions about what electives to offer are made based on students' interests as well as on the skills and knowledge needed in postsecondary education, employment, and life. If the school does not have the resources to offer a course, the staff works to secure the necessary resources.
- Teachers strive to stretch the students in their learning. The school maintains a close relationship with postsecondary institutions and brings in postsecondary teachers to work with the students.
- Diversity is nurtured in this environment, including different approaches and teaching styles, because it reflects what students will encounter in life. This diversity also means that the students can find adults with whom to identify.
- Capacity to meet the needs of students is constantly being developed.
- The administration functions so well, it is invisible.

Sunset Ridge Middle School
Sandy, Utah

Overview

Sunset Ridge Middle School opened its doors in fall 2005. Even before the school opened, the new staff came together in order to create a vision of what the ultimate middle school would look like. They researched how middle school students learn and what structures and practices would best support the vision of the ideal school. Parents were key participants in the creation of this vision. Together, staff and parents took deliberate steps to create the ideal middle school.

Located in the northwest corner of the Jordan School District, Sunset Ridge currently serves 950 students in grades 7 though 9 and has been growing by about 200 students annually. The school building was designed with middle school practices in mind; the classrooms are organized into cross-curricular houses and equipped with the latest instructional technology.

Sunset Ridge recognizes the unique characteristics of middle school students. Staff works to respond to the needs these characteristics create. Students are organized into teams or houses to nurture a sense of security and belonging. Teachers work together to create learning activities that make learning relevant to the real world. Subjects are not studied in isolation, but are connected to answer the often asked question: "Why do I have to know this?" A culture of mutual respect and safety is established. Students are supported in positive risk taking as they learn new skills. Sunset Ridge is a school where trying is rewarded and students are supported to improve.

Program Components

Key to success at the middle level is a clear understanding of the students being served. Implications for the educators who teach these students are enormous and cannot be ignored. High-performing middle schools recognize that middle level students rise to the top when there is *less*:

- less whole-class, teacher-directed learning
- less student passivity: sitting, listening, receiving, and absorbing information
- less prizing and rewarding of silence in the classroom
- less classroom time devoted to fill-in-the blank worksheets, workbooks, and other seat work
- less time spent reading textbooks and basal readers
- less of an attempt by teachers to thinly cover large amounts of material in every subject area
- less rote memorization of facts and details
- less stress on competition and grades in school
- less tracking and ability grouping

- less special pull-out programs
- less use of reliance on standardized tests

Thus, middle school students rise to the top when there is *more*:

- more experiential, hands-on learning
- more active learning, with all the attendant noise and movement of students doing, talking, and collaborating
- more emphasis on higher-order thinking
- more deep study of a smaller number of topics
- more time devoted to reading whole, original, real books and nonfiction materials
- more responsibility transferred to students for their work: goal setting, record keeping

At Sunset Ridge, all students are expected to meet high academic standards. The school's leadership team consists of all department chairs who have worked collaboratively to develop a schoolwide letter of disclosure. The disclosure sets high academic standards for each and every student in every class in the school. Students are held to a standard of "total quality work" and are given multiple opportunities and support to revise their work until the standard is met.

Special education students are included in regular education classes, except for mathematics, in order to give them equal access to the curriculum. Special education teachers work in the classrooms to give the students additional support and make appropriate accommodations. Every student has an adult advocate through the school's teacher advisory program. Grade checks and opportunities to complete missing work are conducted during teacher advisory class times. Teachers work together to regroup students who need additional support for work completion during these make-up days.

Curriculum, instruction, and assessment are aligned with high standards. All teachers must follow the Utah State Core Curriculum. Language arts, social studies, math, and science have collaboratively developed curriculum maps. Departments work to ensure a common curriculum regardless of the individual teacher.

Some departments have participated in vertical teaming with the high school in order to ensure a smooth transition from year to year. These same subjects are developing common assessments at the course level in order to quickly assess student progress and adjust instructional practice.

Instructional practices include a variety of teaching and learning strategies. Teachers work in collaborative teams by grade and by academic department to evaluate and share effective instructional practices focused on the curriculum map standards. Data from the common assessments helps in the sharing of effective instructional practices.

Teachers use a variety of methods to assess student performance and maintain a collection of students' work. Through projects, teachers assess cooperative learning activities, peer review, traditional paper and pencil activities, presentations, and performance tasks. In many cases, rubrics clearly define the performance expectations allowing students to assess their own and others' work. In addition to classroom notebooks, students and teachers work together to create portfolios of work that students present to parents during student-led conferences twice each year. Teachers are beginning to be very reflective about the quality of student assignments and are beginning to question whether each assessment indicates mastery or merely compliance with teacher demands.

The school provides students time to meet rigorous standards. "Total quality work" and "Remediate, Improve, Stretch, and Excel" (RISE) allow students to work until they have achieved the learning objective. They also allow students who have achieved the objective to participate in stretch learning activities. These are accomplished through whole-school flex scheduling and grade-level flex scheduling. We have begun to implement a schoolwide pyramid of interventions in order to provide systemwide support for students who are struggling. Support is given through the teacher advisory class. Parents are informed of academic progress through an online grade program, parent contacts outlined in the pyramid of interventions, and student-led conferences. Small grade-level teams of teachers consistently contact parents as a group when they have concerns about student performance.

Sunset Ridge was founded with a culture of collaboration and is predicated on a sense that it is essential to do whatever it takes on behalf of students. Staff members worked to develop a shared vision and mission statement in order to guide their work. They adopted criteria described by the National Forum to Accelerate Middle Level Reform, and looked to research from other organizations. They also implemented the International Center's 10 Key Components Fundamental to School Improvement. Sunset Ridge continues to use those components as a roadmap to ongoing improvement.

APPENDIX

References

Baldrige National Quality Program. *Criteria for Performance Excellence*. Online: http://www.quality.nist.gov/Criteria.htm

Bringing Best Practices to Scale

Covey, S. *Seven Habits of Highly Effective People*. Free Press, 2004.

Daggett, W.R., Kruse, B. and Kruse, B. *Education is NOT a Spectator Sport*. International Center for Leadership in Education, 1997. *out of print*

Danielson, C. *Enhancing Professional Practice, 2nd edition* Association for Supervision and Curriculum Development (ASCD). 1996.

Howe, N. and Strauss, W. *Millennials Rising – the Next Great Generation*. Vintage, 2000.

I CAN Learn Mathematics program. Online: http://www. icanlearn.com

Kovalik, S. *How Brain Research Impacts Instruction.* International Center for Leadership in Education, 2008.

Kovalik, S. *Highly Effective Teaching Model.*

National Assessment of Educational Progress (NAEP). *Mapping 2005 State Proficiency Standards onto the NAEP Scales,* June 2007.

National Forum to Accelerate Middle Level Reform. Online: http://www.mgforum.org

National Center for Education Statistics. *Mapping 2005 State Proficiency Standards onto the NAEP Scales.* 2007. Online: http://nces.ed.gov/nationsreportcard/pubs/studies/2007482. asp

Scholastic. *READ 180.* Online: http://teacher.scholastic.com/ products/read180